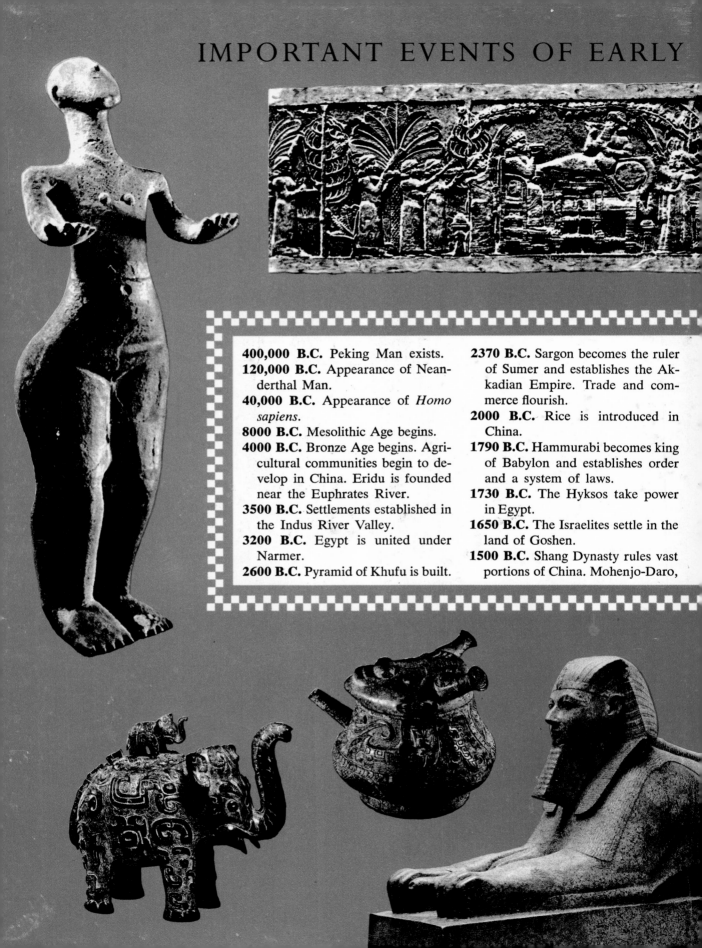

400,000 B.C. Peking Man exists.

120,000 B.C. Appearance of Neanderthal Man.

40,000 B.C. Appearance of *Homo sapiens*.

8000 B.C. Mesolithic Age begins.

4000 B.C. Bronze Age begins. Agricultural communities begin to develop in China. Eridu is founded near the Euphrates River.

3500 B.C. Settlements established in the Indus River Valley.

3200 B.C. Egypt is united under Narmer.

2600 B.C. Pyramid of Khufu is built.

2370 B.C. Sargon becomes the ruler of Sumer and establishes the Akkadian Empire. Trade and commerce flourish.

2000 B.C. Rice is introduced in China.

1790 B.C. Hammurabi becomes king of Babylon and establishes order and a system of laws.

1730 B.C. The Hyksos take power in Egypt.

1650 B.C. The Israelites settle in the land of Goshen.

1500 B.C. Shang Dynasty rules vast portions of China. Mohenjo-Daro,

CIVILIZATIONS 400,000 B.C. - 689 B.C.

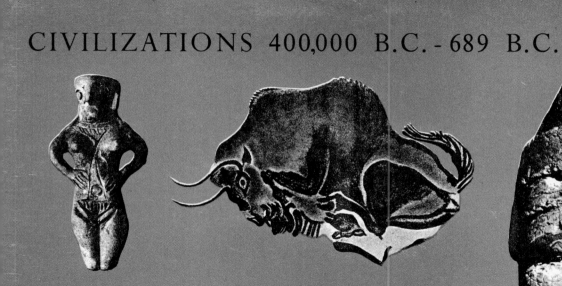

the early capital of India is destroyed by invaders. Queen Hatshepsut rules in Egypt.

1483 B.C. Thutmose III conquers Syria and the Sudan.

1380 B.C. Anyang becomes the capital of the Shang Dynasty.

1375 B.C. Suppiluliumas I becomes king of the Hittites at the height of their power.

1370 B.C. Amenhotep IV (Akhnaton) takes the throne of Egypt with his wife Nefertiti.

1354 B.C. Tutankhamon becomes ruler of Egypt.

1290 B.C. Ramesses II becomes ruler of Egypt.

1286 B.C. The Hittites defeat the Egyptians in the Battle of Kadesh.

1200 B.C. Picture writing emerges in China.

1025 B.C. The Chou Dynasty rules China.

1000 B.C. Hinduism is introduced into India.

930 B.C. Israel established.

705 B.C. Death of Sargon, ruler of Assyria.

689 B.C. Sennacherib of Assyria destroys Babylon.

HISTORY OF

Editor Irwin Shapiro

Associate Editor Jonathan Bartlett

Consultant Albert Fried,
*Department of History,
Queens College, New York*

Contributors Anne Howard Bailey

John Bowman

Ormonde deKay, Jr.

Edith Firoozi

Albert Fried

Johanna Johnston

Ira N. Klein

Willis Lindquist

Edna Ritchie

Seymour Reit

James L. Steffensen

VOLUME I

THE WORLD

EARLY CIVILIZATIONS

by John Bowman

GOLDEN PRESS NEW YORK

CONTENTS

The Coming of Man

11

Primitive man develops after millions of years and begins to use simple tools following the Great Ice Age. Homo sapiens *appears and nomadic tribes settle in permanent communities.*

Where Civilization Began 4000 B.C.-1750 B.C.

20

The Mesopotamian civilizations rise in the valleys of the Tigris and Euphrates Rivers. Agriculture develops, cities are established, and government, religion, and the arts thrive. The great empire of Babylon flourishes.

Hittite Warriors Build a Kingdom 1750 B.C.-700 B.C.

31

The Hittites sweep down from Central Asia, to conquer Turkey and all of Babylonia, but are then driven out by the Assyrians.

The Gift of the Nile 3300 B.C.-30 B.C.   35

The Upper and Lower Kingdoms of the Nile are united and, under a succession of powerful pharaohs, Egypt becomes a great Empire. The Pyramids are built. Finally, conquered in turn by Persia, Alexander the Great, and Rome, Egypt loses its power.

The People of One God 3000 B.C.-30 B.C.   50

Abraham leads his people from Sumer to the Land of Canaan. In a pagan world, the Jews establish a new religion based on a belief in one God. From the teachings of the Jews emerge two other religions, Christianity and Islam.

The Rise of the Assyrians 1600 B.C.-539 B.C.   56

Through its powerful armies, Assyria becomes the dominant power in the Near East. Strong rulers and a tightly-knit government make them rich and powerful until they are conquered by the Babylonians under Nebuchadnezzar.

A New People, a New Faith 650 B.C.-330 B.C.   61

Babylon falls to the Persians. Under Cyrus, Persia dominates the East with its wise rule. Darius extends the Empire from Europe to India, but is finally defeated by Alexander the Great.

Civilization Comes to India 3500 B.C.-200 B.C.   68

A highly sophisticated culture develops along the Indus River, and Hinduism introduces a caste system. After King Asoka binds the areas of India into a loose confederation, Buddhism becomes the religion of the people.

The Land of the Great Wall 4000 B.C.-A.D. 220   80

Originally an agricultural society ruled by tribal chieftains, China becomes an empire under Shih Huan. Under three dynasties, the Shang, Han, and Chou, China is ruled by the Emperor, known as the "Son of Heaven." The Great Wall is built to discourage invaders, and trade and culture thrive. Buddhism becomes the religion of the people; Confucianism that of the upper classes.

Editorial Staff

Irwin Shapiro—*Project Director and Editor-in-Chief*
Albert Fried—*Project Consultant*
Jonathan Bartlett—*Associate Editor*
Jos. Trautwein—*Project Coordinator*

ASSISTANTS

Ian McMahan
James L. Steffensen
Marguerite Raben

Art and Production Staff

Jos. Trautwein—*Project Director*
Ahza Cohen—*Associate Director*
Jeanette Cissman

ASSISTANTS

Alice Popper
Harriet Torjussen

Art

STUDIO HACHETTE, PARIS, FRANCE
Florence de la Villehuchet—*European Coordinator*
Christine Fouret—*Assistant*
Alton Tobey
Carroll Jones
Rudy Zallinger
Steele Savage
George Gross
Morton Jones
Tran Mawicke

Research and Photographs

Ahza Cohen
Ronald Buehl
Olivia Buehl
Peggy Simsarian

FOREWORD

EACH OF US IS A PART OF HISTORY.

More than that, each of us is a maker of history.

Sometimes, as when we cast our vote in an election,

we make history consciously; but always, whether we are aware of it or not,

we are in our daily actions helping to shape the history of our times.

As makers of history, it is of the utmost importance for us to know

the past, which has molded our society, our religions, our

institutions of government, and our ways of thought. And we must know the past

of nations other than our own, for we no longer live in isolated groups.

Today jet planes reach distant lands in hours,

messages are sent in minutes, and sensitive instruments scan the earth from outer space.

The peoples of the world have become our neighbors.

What they do affects us; what we do affects them. We must learn to understand them,

and the key to that understanding is history.

Happily, modern historians have made the reading of history as

pleasurable as it is profitable. They see history not as a mere chronicle of names and

dates and events, but as the story of mankind—a fascinating story,

more adventurous and exciting than any tale imagined by the masters of fiction.

The publishers hope that this series will make the story more accessible

and contribute to our understanding of the world, its people—and ourselves.

THE EDITORS

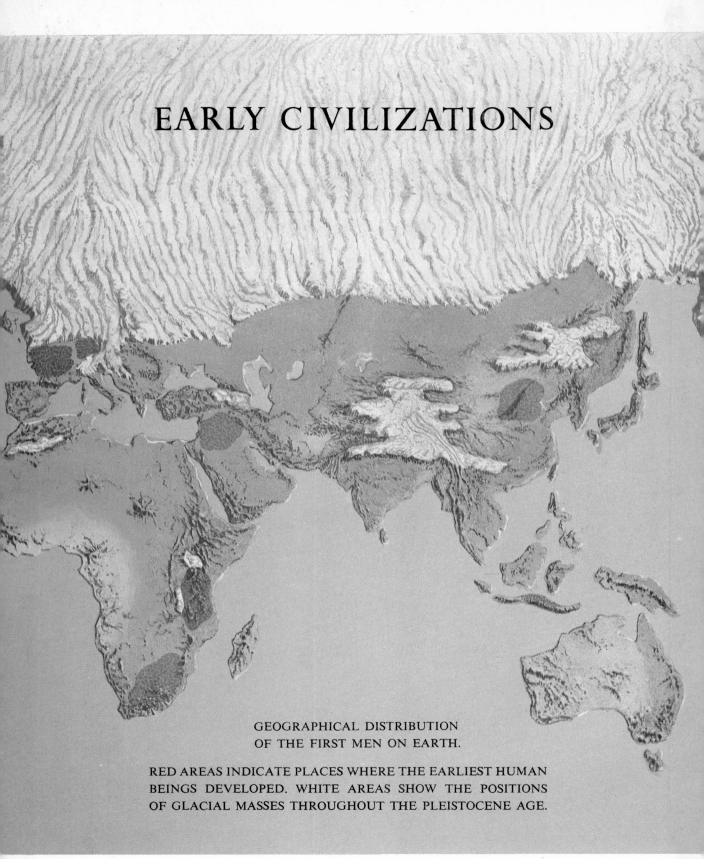

EARLY CIVILIZATIONS

GEOGRAPHICAL DISTRIBUTION
OF THE FIRST MEN ON EARTH.

RED AREAS INDICATE PLACES WHERE THE EARLIEST HUMAN
BEINGS DEVELOPED. WHITE AREAS SHOW THE POSITIONS
OF GLACIAL MASSES THROUGHOUT THE PLEISTOCENE AGE.

The Coming of Man

Prehistory

ABOUT 400,000 years ago, a group of people were gathered at the mouth of a cave. They had a fire in which they were roasting deer meat, and around them lay the bones of monkeys, wild pigs, and water buffalo from previous meals. One of the women was picking berries from the nearby bushes. A man sitting close to the fire chipped away at a broken stone he would use to cut off chunks of the cooked meat. Another man, too hungry to wait, gnawed the marrow from some bones.

11

The cave was one of several not far from what is now Peking, China, and the people who first used these caves are known as Peking Man. Peking Man did not leave anything behind except some bones, charcoal, berries, and stones, but these are enough to suggest certain things about the way he lived. They show that the people at the caves ate meat as well as plants, made crude tools, could kill large animals, and knew how to keep a fire alive.

With fire they could keep warm and fend off wild animals at night. Probably they cooked some foods in the fire. Instead of eating in the fields after killing an animal, the men might wait until they gathered around the fire to eat. Such a meal became something of a family or group occasion. There was a sharing of tasks, of food, of pleasures. No one said much, but with simple language the adults could pass on something of what they had learned to their children.

At times, when food was scarce, these people may have eaten human flesh, but it is likely that they killed only to survive. Or perhaps they believed that by eating human flesh they could obtain the strength of a slain enemy, or keep the spirit of a dead comrade.

Among the things left behind by Peking Man were bones which had been pried open. To pry open a bone takes a certain knowledge and skill; Peking Man must have had an intelligence. As primitive as he was, he belongs to human history.

THE GREAT ICE AGE

It had taken millions of years for a body and a brain to develop and work together as Peking Man's did. But at least 600,000 years before Peking Man appeared, man was already standing erect and grasping tools he himself had made. Man was then near the beginning of the Pleistocene Epoch, a period that takes its name from Greek words meaning "most recent." Although the Pleistocene Epoch began one million years ago, that is considered recent when compared to the many millions of years in the life of the earth.

During the Pleistocene Epoch, there were various types of men at different stages of development. One of the most primitive types was the *Australopithecus*. The name means "southern ape-like" and refers to southern Africa, where many

Then the ice began to melt and the glaciers retreated. Sea levels rose and land bridges between
various areas of higher ground vanished, leaving
some creatures isolated. During these interglacial
periods, the climate often became semi-tropical in
regions where the ice had been. Plants, animals,
and men spread into the new territory.

The last glacial period ended about 11,000 years
ago. But during the hundreds of thousands of
years of the great Ice Age, man was developing as
he moved and changed with the climate. Little has
survived of man during this period, except for
his stone tools. These have given the period its
best-known name, the Paleolithic ("old stone")
Age.

bones of this type have been found. A later and
more advanced type is the *Pithecanthropus,* meaning "apelike man." Peking Man belonged to this
group, along with such relatives as the one found
on the island of Java. Still more advanced types
developed in the years that followed.

During all these years, the earth itself was passing through an ice age. In the early part of the
Pleistocene Epoch, the first of four glacial periods
began. Each lasted many thousands of years and
was followed by a warm interglacial period also
lasting thousands of years. During a glacial period,
large masses of ice moved down from the moun-
tainous regions in the north and across Europe,
Asia, and the Americas. As the great ice masses—
and the cold climate—spread across much of the
northern hemisphere, vegetation was wiped out
and animals were driven southward. Rains moved
across new routes, and the region just north of the
equator became a fertile grassland where animal
life flourished and men tended to concentrate.

EARLY MAN HAD NO PERMANENT HOME.
HE WAS FORCED TO MOVE CONSTANTLY
IN HIS NEVER-ENDING SEARCH FOR FOOD.

BECAUSE OF INTENSE COLD, NEANDERTHAL MAN USED CAVES AS HIS FIRST SHELTERS.

From the beginning, there was the one thing that set man apart from the animals: he changed objects so that he could use them as tools. His first tools were probably wooden clubs and sticks and bones for digging. Soon he saw the advantages of stone and began to break or chip rough edges on pebbles. He discovered, too, that hard stones like flint could be given a sharp edge that penetrated other materials, such as wood, bone, and flesh. In many parts of the world flint became the most common material for tools.

Peking Man did not make anything from stone except crude chopping stones and flakes with rough cutting edges. But in Africa and Europe, men chipped more precisely and put sharp edges on stones. Their basic tool was the hand axe. It had no wooden handle, but the stone was shaped with two sides, cutting edges, and a blunt end. Grasping this blunt end in one hand—or both, since a hand axe might be up to two feet long—a man could perform such tasks as digging, splitting, or butchering.

Gradually, here and there, man began to find new ways of making different kinds of stone tools. In general, tools became smaller, thinner, sharper, and handier. Man went to much trouble to shape a stone. He took pride in a neat job.

"INTELLIGENT MAN" APPEARS

For hundreds of thousands of years, man's advance must be measured by his stone tools. Then, about 120,000 years ago, a different type of man appeared in many parts of the world. This was Neanderthal Man, named after the German valley where his remains were first discovered. Europe had still to pass through the final glacial period, and Neanderthal Man took to living in caves. He hunted animals such as reindeer, musk ox, woolly mammoth, and bear, which were all forced to live at the edge of the glaciers.

Neanderthal Man became a highly skilled stone-chipper and made stone flakes into scrapers and knives. He made points so finely edged that they could penetrate the thick skins of the animals he hunted. Neanderthal Man's life was so involved with animals that he seems to have developed a cult of animal worship. In the arms of a man buried in a cave he placed the jaws of a bear; this suggests that he considered the bear sacred. And, although earlier men may have buried their dead, Neanderthal Man was the first to place food and

NEANDERTHAL MAN LEARNED TO CAPTURE ANIMALS
FOR FOOD AND TO USE THEIR SKINS FOR CLOTHING.

tools with the body. There was a feeling for an afterlife, a sense of religion.

Then, about 40,000 years ago, Neanderthal Man gave way to a new type of man—*Homo sapiens,* or "intelligent man." This was modern man, who appeared in the Near East, North Africa, and Europe. An early type of European modern man is named Cro Magnon Man after the French site where his remains were discovered. Modern man also moved into southeast Asia, into the Far East, and into Australia.

Some of these modern men became the first people in America. Moving out of Asia, they crossed the Bering Strait—perhaps over a bridge of land or ice—to Alaska. Then, pushing forward in search of food, they moved down and across North America, Middle America, and South America. It was many years before modern man reached the barrens of northeastern Canada, or Greenland, or Antarctica, or the mid-Pacific islands, but about 15,000 years ago, modern man had taken over much of the earth's habitable surface.

From the beginning, man had been adapting to conditions such as extreme heat or cold. Different physical features such as skin colors or body types were developing, too. Modern man now became many men, living in different ways throughout the world. For all their differences, however, their lives were much the same and their advances still depended on simple tools.

ABOUT 40,000 YEARS AGO CAME THE FIRST EXAMPLES OF RELIGIOUS FEELING: MYSTERIOUS CULTS OF DEATH AND THE HUNT.

Some men found better ways to make the old tools. They improved the spear by tipping it with points of stone or bone. They invented the spear-thrower, a narrow stick that allowed a man to launch a spear and thus increase its power.

Men were also making new tools. With one, the burin, a chisel-like instrument, a man could make needles out of bone and ivory, and with needles he began to sew clothing from skins and furs. He could then live in colder climates and hunt rein-

CAVE DWELLERS OFTEN PAINTED REMARK-ABLE PICTURES OF MEN AND ANIMALS.

deer, whose antlers provided still another material for tools.

As men moved into new territories, they met new problems, but now they were able to handle them. One group of people, for instance, lived in the flatlands of northern Europe and southern Russia. There were no caves and the climate was severe. The people scraped a few inches of soil off the ground and then erected a roof of animal skins or branches covered with dirt. Inside this dwelling they had a fire, and in this way they survived to hunt the great mammoths.

It was a hard life, and yet these people took time to make themselves ornaments, such as beads, bracelets, and pins. They decorated ivory and bone objects with simple geometric designs, and carved small stone or ivory figurines, apparently for a religious cult. Man was already giving thought to things beyond his immediate needs.

As the last glacial period drew to an end in Europe, a mild climate settled in, and along with it came various kinds of wild game. Hunters began to live in and around the many caves and rock shelters of southwestern France and northern Spain. Here, in the caves, men began to paint.

In different caves, at different times, they painted with their fingers or simple brushes. Sometimes they blew dry powdered paint onto a surface prepared with fat. Sometimes they shaded in figures with black, sometimes with a color, and sometimes with several colors. Between 20,000 and 10,-000 years ago, men were covering the walls and ceilings of caves with an astonishing variety of forms, mostly of men and animals.

The artists did not paint these pictures merely to show their skill or to give pleasure. The paintings were part of the magic and religious beliefs of people whose survival depended on these animals. The people believed that the pictures were a link with the forces behind the fertility of the animals and the success of the hunters. The cave was a sacred place, or sanctuary, and at some stage the paintings may have been used as part of a ritual. Perhaps, in the depths of the caves, by the light of fires and torches, there was dancing and chanting. Men in animal skins and masks may have performed, for such figures are painted on the walls of some of the caves.

The way of life of such hunters lasted for many years in some parts of the world. In other parts of the world, men entered a period of great change. This happened about 10,000 years ago, when the final glacial period came to an end and the climate that was to mark modern times developed. The period of change is known as the Mesolithic ("middle stone") Age. Since it fell within quite recent times, it can be dated as beginning about 8000 B.C. Depending on the people and the region, the Mesolithic Age lasted from one thousand to several thousand years.

HUNTERS AND FOOD GATHERERS

During this period, men began to find new ways of obtaining food besides hunting and food-gathering. Some people had long eaten shellfish, but shore dwellers now began to eat them as a staple. Men learned how to spear fish and how to make hooks, nets, and even dugout canoes. Later they made harpoons and hunted seals or caught stranded whales.

When men could feed themselves from the sea, new areas opened up for settlement. Men also began to move into woodlands, with their fresh materials for shelters and food. The old cutting tools were inefficient, and soon men were making an axe with a handle. Later they began to polish the axe blade with abrasives like sand, giving an edge that cut neater and faster. Men also began to make tiny chips of stone that could be set into other materials to provide jagged cutting edges.

Men still remained hunters, but now they had two new aids—the dog and the bow and arrow. The ancestors of dogs had been coming and going

MESOLITHIC MAN FIRST USED THE BOW AND VARIOUS IMPLEMENTS AND TOOLS OF BONE.

around campfires for some time. About 10,000 years ago, dogs were already men's hunting companions and were used for tracking, cornering, and retrieving game. The bow and arrow had no ancestors in nature but was a true invention, combining several parts and principles. At first it aided man the hunter; later it served man the warrior.

Despite such changes, most people remained hunters and food gatherers who stayed close to rock shelters wherever the search for food took them. Wood, stone, and bone were still the basic mate-

AS THE CLIMATE GREW WARM, MAN BEGAN TO CONSTRUCT HUTS AND FORM VILLAGES.

17

rials for tools. Then something new appeared in the Near East. In the region that stretched from Palestine, up across Turkey, and down into Iraq, the highland plains and valleys supported a rich variety of small game and wild plants. Life did not have to be organized around hunting a few large animals, and the climate enabled men to relax a bit. A few people here began to make sickles to cut grasses and grains. Some people also made grinding mills and pounding stones to prepare the wild grains they gathered.

Men had long known where and when certain wild grasses and plants grew best. Perhaps they had even tended the fields by driving away animals and pulling out unwanted plants. After the grains were gathered, men learned how to prepare them. It was the people of the Near East who took the next step. Perhaps someone accidentally dropped some seeds, forgot about them, and only later noticed some grain growing in the area. Or perhaps people returned to an old campsite and saw a good growth of grain where their garbage had

been thrown. Most likely it was the women who noticed such things, since the men were too busy hunting to worry about a few stalks of grain. But when people learned that grains could be made to grow where they wanted them, farming began.

METALS AND INVENTIONS

The people of the Near East at first grew wild barley and wheat, but soon they were cultivating many wild vegetables and fruits. They also began to use such tools as the sickle, the hoe and, later, the plow. In time, too, men in the Near East learned how to irrigate their fields. Knowledge of how to farm spread to other regions and had a great effect on the life of the people at that time. Meanwhile, people in southeast Asia had begun on their own to cultivate other kinds of plants, and the Indians of Middle America had started to grow a primitive kind of corn. Later, the American Indians would be the first to cultivate many other

FARMING WAS THE BASIS OF VILLAGE LIFE.

plants such as the potato, tomato, pumpkin, and peanut.

The way of life that began to develop with farming marked a new period, the Neolithic ("new stone") Age. As with the preceding periods, the name refers to the tools made by the peoples of this time. The complete neolithic culture, however, included many other developments besides tools. By this time, for instance, some men were building their own houses, with roofs, pavements, fireplaces, and storage pits. They even built special rooms for their gods and religious rituals. Men were becoming village and town dwellers, and at Jericho, in Palestine, they built town walls with a tower. Along with their farming and settlements, neolithic men were domesticating animals. Sheep, goats, pigs, and cattle were first used in their half-wild state, and then men began to breed them in captivity. Later, men began to milk such animals as goats and cattle.

In their settlements, people were learning how to shape new materials. Perhaps a woman noticed that a basket lined with mud became hard and waterproof after standing near a fire or beneath the sun. Before long many people were making pots of every size and shape and decorating them with surface marks or paints. Neolithic people also began to spin and weave and developed the loom. This provided more materials for clothing, and also turned some men from hunting to cultivating flax and cotton and tending sheep for wool.

Farming, villages, domesticated animals, pottery, weaving—these made up the neolithic culture that the people of the Near East had taken the lead in developing. Soon the new ways were being adopted by other people, who learned about them from migrant groups or from individual travelers and traders. Not all people took over all the new ways, and each group adapted the new ways to its own conditions. But the basic neolithic culture was taken up by much of mankind around the Mediterranean and in Africa, Europe, central Asia, India, and the Far East.

Meanwhile, in the highlands of Turkey and Iran, another development took place. A few men began to smelt copper from ore. By 5000 B.C. they were making small ornaments and tools, and soon they were making bowls. By smelting other earths and rocks, men discovered metals such as silver, tin, and lead. Bronze, a mixture of tin and copper, was probably discovered by an accidental smelting of an ore mixture. Stone and pottery continued to be the basic materials for a long time; metal was

MANY SETTLERS NEAR THE WATER USED BOATS AS A MEANS OF TRANSPORTATION.

for only a few privileged persons. Still, once metal-working started, it developed and spread.

While this was going on during several thousand years, still other discoveries were giving man new sources of energy. For a long time, man had depended largely on his own muscle. Only recently had he hitched animals to plows and sledges, and some men were getting work out of the ass, the reindeer, the horse, and the camel. Now, with the invention of the wheel, men could move themselves and large loads over the land quite easily. With the sail, men could move ships. Simple applied mechanics, too, enabled men to haul water or move great weights. For a long time to come, manpower continued to do most of the work, whether it was building the pyramids of Egypt or hauling large stones to Stonehenge, but a new world was opening up.

Even before metals or the wheel affected most men's lives, a more basic change took place in the neolithic world. Men were able to produce a surplus of food to support people such as priests and craftsmen, who did tasks other than farming. In a settlement where goods and labor were exchanged, there was a need to keep accounts and generally to administer the community's property and activities. Out of such communities grew the civilizations that would make history, and from their simple records came the writing to record that history.

Where Civilization Began

4000 B.C. - 1750 B.C.

By 4000 B.C., many different groups of people were working out their lives in a variety of ways. In a great arc from the eastern coast of the Mediterranean, across the Turkish plains, and through the highlands of Iraq and Iran, groups of peoples had settled and were farming, tending animals, making pottery, and building towns, markets, and forts. In the deserts, mountains, and steppes, nomadic tribesmen lived by herding animals, and by hunting and raiding. As all these populations grew, they began to compete for land, food, and supplies.

One of the areas that was to become most sought after was a stretch of land almost at the very center of these various peoples. It was only about 150 miles wide and 600 miles long, and extended from the foothills of northwestern Iraq to the Persian Gulf. Two rivers, the Tigris and the Euphrates, drained the area and gave it its name, Mesopotamia —"the land between the rivers."

For the next 3,500 years, Mesopotamia was to witness the rise and fall of many cities and cultures. Sumerians, Akkadians, Babylonians, Assyrians, Chaldaeans—these were only some of the people who took root and flourished in this land. Finally the Persians came and reduced Mesopotamia to a mere province. But from the first unknown settlers to the mighty Nebuchadnezzar, this land gave rise to much that would affect all civilization.

The first settlers in Mesopotamia set up their villages and farmed in the upper reaches of the Tigris. These were among the earliest farming communities anywhere in the world, but they gradually declined and it was many years later before this region came to be known as Assyria.

Mesopotamia's southern region, which was later called Babylonia, was especially hot and dry and did not seem to attract early man. But between the rivers were broad plains, ideal for farming if

they could be watered. Along the lower reaches, and in the delta, were marshlands with fish and wild fowl, and reeds that could be made into boats and huts. What was needed to develop this territory were men willing to settle and work the land.

THE FOUNDING OF ERIDU

For a long time, people came and went in southern Mesopotamia. Then, about 4000 B.C., men from the east settled at a site called Eridu, in the delta near the Euphrates River. They farmed and fished and made pottery. Stone was so rare that they even baked clay tools. There was not enough rainfall to support their crops, but the fertile lands along the river were easily flooded. To keep the marshes drained and to bring water to more and distant fields, men began to develop a system of dikes and canals. The construction and upkeep of such an irrigation system took much planning and labor, and men were forced to work together. True community living had begun.

Soon the community at Eridu built itself a shrine to its patron god. It was a simple building, made of the same unbaked bricks used for their

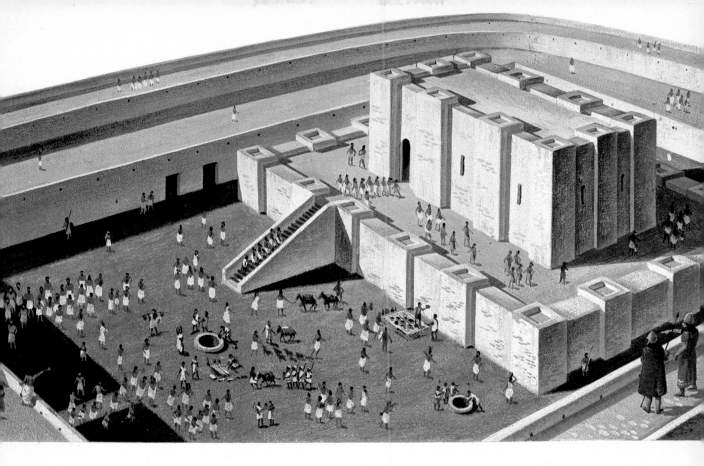

houses. This was only proper, since the shrine was the home of the god. Inside, on its altar, people laid their offerings of fish and other foods to express thanks for past harvests and hopes for the future. If the god became unhappy, he might leave the city and expose it to evils and enemies.

As the community grew, there was need for more food. The irrigation system was enlarged, but the floods in the delta and marshlands were so unpredictable and destructive that people began to settle farther up on the plains. North of Eridu, for instance, there was the prosperous city of Uruk. Its people were not only farmers, but carpenters, priests, and metalsmiths. They also wove cloth, made fine stone carvings, and played music on a simple harp.

THE RISE OF SUMER

No matter how busy they were, the people of Uruk always took time to worship their god. As at Eridu, they periodically built a new temple, using the old building material as its foundation. Now that Uruk was thriving, the great platform towered forty feet above the plain. Stairs and ramps led up to the white temple on the top, where there was an altar to Anu, the great royal sky god. In a city as large and as wealthy as Uruk, there was room for other gods and temples as well.

This southernmost part of Mesopotamia was called Sumer, and now many cities were growing there. Along with Eridu and Uruk, there were Ur, Lagash, and Nippur, each with its own supreme god and other minor gods. Some of the gods were recognized by all Sumerians. Among them were Anu, the sky god, and his son Enlil, lord of wind and earth; Ea, god of water; and Nanna, or Sin, the moon god who governed the night, the months, and the calendar. All Sumerians also worshiped Uta, or Shamash, the sun god. Since he was "the one from whom no secrets are hid," Uta was also the god of justice.

Each god had his temple home in one city or another, often on a high platform, or ziggurat. The ziggurat was like an artificial mountain rising from the flatlands. The Sumerians called it "the house of the mountain," or "the bond between heaven and earth." To them, all nature—plants, animals, water, even the sun—sprang from the mountains, and it seemed that the life-giving gods would be most at home in a high place.

ATOP THE SACRED TOWERS THE SUMER-
IANS CALLED ZIGGURATS, PRIESTS
OFFERED SACRIFICES TO THE GODS.

The temple that towered over the city was the center of the city's life. All land was considered the estate of the god, with the high priest acting as the god's steward. As farming and irrigation became more complicated, officials were appointed to supervise the work. In time, some citizens gained control of large lots of land and became wealthy. Other people became so indebted that they had to sign themselves into slavery. At all times, however, everyone worked for the good of the community.

The area around the temple was a busy place. Here were brought the various products—grains, vegetables, fish, cheeses, dates, sesame seed, wool, skins, reeds. Some of the products were given to support the temple staff and the community's festivals. Some were stored for famine and emergencies, or distributed among those who could not farm, or exported to other cities and distant tribes.

Supervising all this were the various men who combined the roles of temple priests and civic officials. Quotas had to be filled, land assigned, goods divided. A system for keeping records was needed, and it was not long before the Sumerians were working with numbers. They had two systems, in fact; one was based on the number 60 and the other on the number 10. They could make various calculations and even worked with fractions. Systems of weights and measures were developed at the same time.

WRITING WITH SIGNS

A man could make simple calculations in his head, but certain records had to be kept to administer the community's property. People began to scratch the numbers in stone or press them in clay tablets. Alongside the numbers they drew outlines of the objects accounted for—livestock, human heads, plants, tools, buildings. Soon they began to simplify the pictures, eliminating details and leaving little more than a sign.

They soon realized that a drawing or sign could stand for something beyond itself. The sign for star came to mean "heaven," the sign for foot came to mean "going." After a while, they began to use a sign for its sound alone. The word for arrow, *Ti,* sounded like the word for "life," so a simple arrowhead was used to express a complicated idea. Later the arrowhead was combined with other signs to form words with the *Ti* sound in them.

23

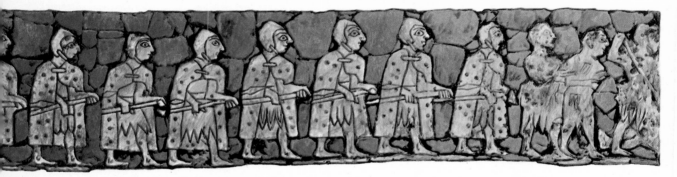

THIS ANIMATED BATTLE SCENE WAS PAINTED BETWEEN 3000 AND 2000 B.C.

For hundreds of years, these signs were used mainly to record lists of produce, receipts of goods, quotas, and rations. The few people who kept such records did not see themselves as creating anything special. They took the clay that was readily at hand and pressed on it with a piece of pointed reed. But the fact is that these early Sumerians had invented writing.

It was the people of Uruk who took the lead in developing writing and other forms of Sumerian culture. But other cities were also advancing, each independent and yet sharing the Sumerian way of life. The rivers made communication and trade easy, and a city might send out a whole colony to watch over trading routes. From the mountains of Iran to the east, the Sumerians got stone, timber, and metals in exchange for their grains. They traded with peoples who lived as far away as Troy and the Caspian Sea. Even the Egyptians learned new ways of doing things from trading with the Sumerians.

RELIGION AND THE GODS

Wherever they went, the Sumerians carried their cylinder seals—semi-precious stones no larger than a finger joint. Carved on each was a design, usually of animals and plants, often done with great artistry. Rolled across wet clay, the design was transferred and became a signature and a seal. To peo-

THIS SUMERIAN TABLET SHOWS ONE
OF THE EARLIEST FORMS OF WRITING.

ple who believed the gods watched over all their doings, it was a curse to disturb a man's seal.

The Sumerians saw nothing strange about calling on the gods to watch over property. Every object, every activity belonged to some god. Besides the great gods of the temples, there were also the gods in the forces of nature—fire, sandstorms, lightning and thunder, the plague. All around men, too, were ghosts, demons, devils, and monsters. Rabiscu the Croucher lurked in doorways and dark corners. Another demon threatened women in childbirth.

Men could do several things to keep the gods and demons happy. The great temple gods were honored with offerings and ceremonies. People wore magic charms or amulets, and in their homes they kept figures of clay or wood. When a man was troubled, he asked a priest or magician to work spells or perform rites. Everything that happened was a possible sign or omen. "If a scorpion lurks in a man's bed, that man shall have riches," went one saying. "If the black winged ants are in town, there will be pouring rain and floods," said another. There was a right way and a wrong way to do everything, and Sumerians had to watch all their actions.

It was religion—the gods, the temples, the priests—that guided the community through all these dangers. Yet, as time went on, life began to change. In the early days, people looked to the temple for leadership in all affairs. The En, the highest official, was both high priest and king. Gradually the En had given up his priestly duties to concentrate on administering the expanding city. The temple, of course, still controlled the land and the farmers who worked it. The ceremonies presided over by the priests and priestesses were still of great importance, and a strong king could still dominate the religious life of his people.

One of the greatest of the priest-kings was Gilgamesh of Uruk. For hundreds of years afterwards, men throughout the Near East told tales that made him seem more like a god than a man. Gilgamesh performed superhuman feats to protect Uruk, but one day he began to fear death. He set forth to consult an ancestor, Utnapishtim, who had been made immortal. After a long and dangerous journey, Gilgamesh found Utnapishtim, and asked him how he had been freed from the threat of death.

Utnapishtim was willing enough to tell the story. The gods had once decided to wipe out all mankind by a great flood, but the god Ea, who often favored men, warned Utnapishtim and told him

SUMERIAN CRAFTS-MEN DECORATED THIS HARP WITH A CARVED BULL'S HEAD.

to make a ship. Utnapishtim built a large ark, on which he loaded his family, certain craftsmen, various animals, and his treasures. When the earth was flooded, all other life was wiped out. The ark grounded on a mountain peak, and when the water began to go down, Utnapishtim prepared a sacrifice to the gods. It was after this that he and his wife were given the immortality of the gods.

For Gilgamesh, there was to be no such escape from death. Knowing that he must die, he returned

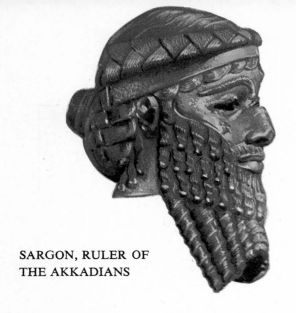

SARGON, RULER OF
THE AKKADIANS

It began with the Sacred Marriage at the temple. This was a traditional ritual, held every year to ensure fertility to the land. This year, however, the sacred couple left the temple and marched down into a burial pit many feet below the ground. They were accompanied by priests, members of the court, musicians, soldiers, and servants. Many of them wore jewelry or carried weapons and treasures. Four-wheeled chariots drawn by oxen were also in the procession.

When they had all gathered in the pit, another ceremony took place. The sacred couple was put to death and buried in a stone chamber. Then dozens of their attendants drank a poisonous drug and lay down to await death. After the oxen were sacrificed and the final rites performed, the whole tomb was filled with earth. It was a royal burial such as only the gods could inspire.

"WHO IS KING?"

Sumerian cities could not afford such extravagant ceremonies very often, yet their gods did seem to be pleased. Then, about 2370 B.C., Sargon, an official of the king of Kish, seized power. A new ruler was not unusual, but Sargon and his followers were Semites, people from the lands to the west.

The Semites had come and gone in Mesopotamia from the beginning, sometimes as migrant groups, sometimes as individuals. Some had settled just north of Sumer in a region known as Akkad. These Semites shared a common past with the Sumerians. They had no interest in doing away with Sumerian culture, and they even took over the Sumerian writing system for their own language, Akkadian.

When Sargon and his Akkadians took over, then, it was more like a change in government. He set up a new capital at Agade and proceeded to take control of many of the cities of Mesopotamia. He destroyed the city walls and put his own people in power. Through trade he extended his influence into Syria and the region along the Mediterranean.

Sargon's descendants expanded his empire. His grandson Naram-Sin defeated various tribes on the edges of Mesopotamia. To guard the trade routes with Turkey and Syria, great forts were built. Some goods went as far as Cyprus and India. Agade, the capital, became a splendid city, with people from all over the world bringing trade and tribute. Elephants and apes were displayed in captivity.

to Uruk, where his last pleasure was to look out over the city and the fortified walls he had helped to build.

Such a tale told a great deal about the Sumerians themselves. It showed their respect for a great priest-king and their pride in the city. It contained the memory of the great floods that had wiped out earlier settlements, and recognition of the fate that awaited all men.

The tale revealed, too, that Uruk had built a wall during the reign of Gilgamesh. Other Sumerian cities such as Ur, Nippur, Lagash, and Kish had also built walls, and they had enlarged their armies as well. They needed to protect themselves from the nomadic tribesmen to the west and the marauding mountainmen to the east. Besides, the cities were competing with each other for land, water rights, and trade routes, and sometimes rivalry broke out into open warfare.

Meanwhile, the king of each city was becoming more powerful. He was taking over the duties of the military chief, who had formerly been elected to lead a city's troops only during some emergency. Now the king was the permanent commander of the army and even passed the position on to his descendants.

No matter how powerful the ruler or how rich the city, the gods were not forgotten. Ur, for instance, was now a wealthy city, with a strong army and a firmly established dynasty of kings. Yet, as in the old days, men still made great sacrifices for their religion. Ur even observed rituals in which several people were buried along with many treasures. Then, on one occasion, about the year 2500 B.C., the king ordered a ceremony more lavish than any before.

SARGON AND HIS
QUEEN IN AGADE

About a century after Sargon founded it, the Akkadian empire began to fall apart. Tribes from the west and the east were raiding the Akkadians, and the Sumerian cities no longer supported their overlords. Then Agade was destroyed, so completely that it would never rise again. With Agade ruined, there was no clear authority. "Who is king?" the people asked. "Who is not king!" came the answer. The Mesopotamian cities fell to the Gutians, barbarous tribesmen from the mountains of Iran. Trade, communications, irrigation were all disrupted. The temples were plundered and famine spread across the land.

By about 2100 B.C., however, Ur had revived and became Sumer's strongest city. Its ruler Ur-Nammu and his descendants formed Ur's third dynasty, which led Ur through a period of great splendor. Ur built itself a ziggurat almost 70 feet high and encouraged the building of cities, temples, and canals throughout Sumer and Akkad. By trade, diplomacy, and military expeditions, Ur extended its influence beyond Mesopotamia. It was not so large an empire as that of Sargon and the Akkadians, but it was more tightly organized.

Administering such an empire required a great many records and documents. Clay tablets and a reed stylus were still the basic materials of the scribes who did the writing, but much had changed since the early days. The signs now in use mostly represented sounds, and all words and ideas could be expressed in writing. Each sign, moreover, had long been reduced to a simple wedge shape, or cuneiform, that could be quickly pressed into the clay. Even so, to become a scribe took many years of training in a scribal school, or "tablet-house." The student who misbehaved or did careless exercises was punished. Families competed with one another to get their children into such schools, for the skill of writing assured a person of a respected career.

Despite its organization, Ur's empire began to

DETAIL OF THE CODE OF HAMMURABI

fall away. Other cities stopped paying tribute, and raiding tribes swooped down on its fortresses, lands, and crops. The final blow came when the Elamites, a people from the southeast, captured Ur and destroyed it. The Sumerian culture had made an impression on Mesopotamia that could never be wiped out; the language would survive for centuries in religious and learned writings. But the power of the Sumerians was ended.

The Elamites did not settle and build an empire. Instead, the Amorites, Semitic tribesmen from the western deserts, took over the cities and set up their kingdoms. For the next two centuries, there was no real central authority in Mesopotamia. Marauders and nomads came and went. In the north, the Assyrians began to show their strength. Various cities took turns trying to rule Mesopotamia, but none succeeded for long.

THE LAWS OF HAMMURABI

Finally, out of all this turmoil, one of the Amorite kings emerged as a true ruler. He was Hammurabi of Babylon, an old Sumerian city that had never been of much importance. But when Hammurabi came to its throne about 1790 B.C., Babylon was becoming one of the stronger cities. Hammurabi took firm control, defeated various warring groups, and gradually brought the cities and lands of Sumer and Akkad into a kingdom of Babylonia.

Hammurabi was more than a military chieftain. He ran a true government, undertaking everything from new canals to a revised calendar. He personally supervised the affairs of his kingdom and was constantly sending letters and documents to his officials. Nothing was too small for his attention. If an official neglected to clear out an irrigation canal, Hammurabi ordered him to do the job and report back. If there was a charge of bribery, Hammurabi ordered an investigation and had everyone involved brought before him.

Hammurabi's great achievement was restoring law and order to the land. He was following tradition when he did this, for the settled peoples of Mesopotamia had always respected law, whether in the conduct of their business or in the worship of their gods. Justice was "the straight thing" that kept people on the right path.

Hammurabi issued many laws and regulations. They dealt with everything from prices, wages, and debts to broken contracts and the conduct of lawsuits. Then, when his reign was drawing to an

BABYLON, METROPOLIS
OF THE MIDDLE EAST

end, he decided that the laws needed improving. Some had to be completely revised; others needed to be explained. With the inspiration of Shamash, god of the sun and of justice, he drew up the new laws. He had them engraved on stone and sent them forth throughout the kingdom.

"Hammurabi, the reverent god-fearing prince," began the inscription, was called by the gods "to make justice appear in the land, to destroy the evil and wicked that the strong might not oppress the weak." The laws that followed dealt with many matters: the administration of justice, property, marriage, assault, agriculture, wages, and slaves. Many of them were based on the ancient idea of "an eye for an eye"—that is, a man who had put out someone's eye would be punished by having his own eye put out. "If a man accuses another man of murder and it proves to be false, the accuser shall be put to death," said one of Hammurabi's

laws. Another said, "If a builder makes a house for a man and the house falls down and causes the death of the owner, the builder shall be put to death." It was harsh justice, but at least the laws were written down for all men to appeal to, and behind them was the power of the king in Babylon.

When Hammurabi died, he was succeeded by his son, but the dynasty soon ended. Kassites, tribesmen from the Zagros Mountains to the east, began to raid Babylonia, and in time they captured the cities of Ur and Uruk. The people in the southern marshes known as the "sea lands" revolted and set up their own kingdom. Then out of the north came a new band of marauders, the Hittites. They took Babylon, plundered and burned it, and then withdrew. But the damage was done. The irrigation systems, writing, the ziggurats, the laws—such things survived for centuries, but the first great age of Mesopotamia was at an end.

Hittite Warriors Build a Kingdom

1750 B.C. - 700 B.C.

AS MASTERS OF THE MIDDLE EAST, HITTITE WARRIORS MADE HATTUSAS, A GREAT FORTIFIED CITY, THEIR CAPITAL.

WITHIN 150 years after the death of Hammurabi, the cities of Mesopotamia were powerless, and other peoples took up the struggle for the Near Eastern world. Among them were the Hittites, who had taken the city of Babylon. The rough Hittite tribesmen hardly knew what to do with such a splendid city, let alone with an empire, so they went back to their strongholds in the highland plains of central Turkey. They had been living there for several centuries, ever since they had left their homeland in the steppes of central Asia.

When the Hittites first moved into Turkey, they had found a land of peasants and small city-states unable to unite in resistance. The Hittites allowed the people to keep their own gods and languages, recruited officials to manage affairs, and left the farmers and craftsmen to their work. It was a bleak, rocky land, hot and dry in summer, cold and windswept in winter. But there were grains and cattle, and the people made beer and wine and kept bees for honey. The land was rich in metal ores, too, and later the Hittites were among the first to use iron.

The Hittites set themselves over the native peoples as an aristocratic warrior class. For many years, rival Hittite tribes and chieftains fought among themselves before Labarnas established himself as the first true king. He led the Hittites in expanding their power throughout Turkey, and his son Hattusilis I extended it into Syria.

Hattusilis made the city of Hattusas his capital. It was strategically located near the crossroads of the main trade routes in central Turkey. As his reign neared its end, Hattusilis could take pride in the kingdom he was leaving to his people, but he had one unpleasant task to perform. He had raised his nephew as his heir, and the boy had proved to be ungrateful. In anger and sorrow, the aged Hattusilis wrote in his will: I, the king, called him my son, embraced him, exalted him, and cared for him continually. But he showed himself a youth not fit

31

to be seen. He shed no tears, he showed no pity, he was cold and heartless. Hattusilis then named his grandson Mursilis as his successor.

It was Mursilis who led the raid on Babylon. When he returned to Hattusas, he was assassinated, and once again various Hittite families and chieftains fought among themselves for the throne. Gradually, however, laws were set down and order was restored. The laws of the Hittites, in fact, were among the best of their time. They called for strict punishment, but it was not always the "eye for an eye" of the Babylonians.

THE HITTITES TRIUMPH

All this time the Hittites were barely able to keep from being wiped out by neighboring tribes. The greatest threat came from the kingdom of Mitanni to the southeast. But the Hittites remained independent, and from their Mitanni enemies they even learned about trained horses and chariots. The Hittites soon became masters at using the horse-drawn chariot in battle and regained much of their former territory.

Under Suppiluliumas I, who became king about 1375 B.C., the Hittites reached the height of their power. He strengthened the Hittite kingdom within Turkey, defeated the Mitanni kingdom, and took over most of Syria. He called himself "the great king, King of the Hittite Land, the hero, the favorite of the Weathergod." His people did indeed look upon him as a hero, and foreign rulers respected him as much for his diplomacy as for his conquests. The widow of an Egyptian Pharaoh even proposed to marry one of his sons.

Hattusas, the capital, was now a great fortified city. It was enclosed by massive walls, some four miles around, with towers and tunnels. Carved sphinxes and lions guarded the gateways, and within the city were temples with dozens of storerooms. In the royal library were thousands of clay tablets recording all the administrative and diplomatic affairs, the laws, literature, history, correspondence, and royal proclamations.

In the hills outside Hattusas was the sacred area of Yazilikaya, with its ceremonial buildings leading into the sanctuary beneath the cliffs. Carved on the rocks were figures of gods and men. During religious festivals, the king led the procession up to Yazilikaya, for he was high priest as well as supreme ruler. He spent part of each year traveling about his kingdom to preside over various religious ceremonies.

The Hittites had hundreds of gods involved in every part of their lives. Chief among them was an old Hittite god, the Weather god, but the Hittites had adopted many of the gods of the peoples they had come in contact with. The Hittites were a practical people who never hesitated to borrow anything from their subjects and neighbors. They were especially influenced by the peoples of Mesopotamia in law, religion, art, medicine, and astrology, and even took over the story of Gilgamesh.

They borrowed words freely, too, although they had their own language, an early version of the languages later to be spoken throughout much of the West. The Hittites developed their own pic-

ture-writing, somewhat like Egyptian hieroglyphs, but this was used mainly for inscriptions carved on monuments. For business and diplomacy they took over the cuneiform script of Mesopotamia, using the wedge-shaped signs to write in their own language on clay tablets. In their dealings with foreign peoples, the Hittites often used Akkadian, the old Semitic language of Mesopotamia.

TREATY WITH THE EGYPTIANS

The successors of Suppiluliumas I fought to hold his empire, but during the reign of his grandson Muwatallis a new threat appeared. The Egyptians under Ramesses II decided to force the Hittites out of Syria. In 1286 B.C. the two great powers met at Kadesh, in northern Syria. Each army numbered about 20,000 men and was led by its king. The Egyptians later charged that Muwatallis had tricked them with two Hittites who pretended to be deserters and said the Hittites had retreated. This put the Egyptians off guard, and the Hittite chariots, in a series of maneuvers, swept down on the Egyptian infantry. Even when a horse was speared, the falling horse and chariot crushed the Egyptian soldiers.

The Hittites won the first battle, but the soldiers stopped to plunder the enemy camp and the Egyptians were able to counterattack. Later, the Egyptians carved the story of the battle of Kadesh on monuments and claimed total victory. The truth was that the Hittites not only stopped the Egyptians but went on to win more territory in Syria.

THE EGYPTIANS LOST THE BATTLE OF KADESH TO THE HITTITES, BUT LATER FALSELY CLAIMED A GREAT VICTORY.

Finally the Hittites and Egyptians came to respect each other's strength, and in 1269 B.C. they made a treaty. They agreed not to attack each other, and to come to each other's defense. It was an important event in international affairs. The treaty was engraved on a silver plaque, the Egyptians carved its text on walls, and the Hittites copied it in cuneiform on tablets for the royal library. Later, the Pharaoh Ramesses II married a Hittite princess, and for many years there was peace in the Near East.

But there were new forces stirring in the west; the peoples of eastern Europe and the Mediterranean were on the move. Among them were the Phry-gians, who swept across Turkey. About 1200 B.C., the Hittite capital, Hattusas, was destroyed and other cities were wiped out. Some Hittites migrated south to their Syrian cities, but the Hittites were no longer a power.

For several centuries afterwards, Syrian city-states such as Carchemish and Karatepe kept up some of the Hittite culture, using Hittite picture-writing on their monumental carvings. Like the older Hittites, they borrowed from many other peoples, including the Egyptians, the Mesopotamians, and the Phoenicians, but they lacked the energy of their ancestors. By 700 B.C., these Syrian city-states were all taken over by the Assyrians.

THE ASSYRIAN FORTRESS AT ZENJIRLI

The Gift of the Nile
3300 B.C.-30 B.C.

RAMESSES II, THE EGYPTIAN RULER WHO BUILT THE FAMOUS TEMPLE AT ABU SIMBEL (1200 B.C.)

IT was around 3300 B.C. and, as it did every year about the middle of July, the Nile had begun to rise. Carrying tons of soil, the waters poured down from the mountains of Africa, where rain and melting snow fed the streams that surged northward into one great river. Wherever it ran free of the rocky canyons, the river overflowed onto the dry fields along its banks. It lapped against the villages on high ground and spread to market towns on the edge of the desert. Moving northward, the river engulfed the entire Delta region, and then emptied into the Mediterranean Sea. By mid-November the waters had receded, leaving a thick, dark mud on the fields and in the canals.

Near one of the largest towns far up the Nile, the farmers stood waiting at the edge of the fields. Then from the town came the king, followed by guards, priests, and servants carrying large fans. The king wore a high white crown and carried a hoe. Scooping some fresh mud out of an irrigation ditch, he placed it in a basket held by an attendant. While the priests chanted, the mud was spread over the field. Now the farmers could plant in the fertile earth left by the floodwaters. The king, who was responsible for the well-being of his people, had performed his duty.

As his white crown indicated, this king ruled only in Upper Egypt. In the Delta to the north there was another king, who wore a red crown. For many years the people of Upper and Lower Egypt had been fighting and raiding each other's towns. But they all had common ancestors who had come from Africa to the south, from Libya to the west, and from Asia to the north and east. Through thousands of years these peoples had mingled in the Nile valley, until finally they had become one people, the Egyptians.

A.

B.

EXAMPLES OF THE HIGHLY DEVELOPED ART OF THE EGYPTIANS

A. EBONY CARVING OF COURT
OFFICIAL, 2000 B.C.

B. BOOK OF THE DEAD (DETAIL)
PAPYRUS, 1500 B.C.

For almost 3,000 years, Egypt remained two lands. Upper Egypt was little more than the narrow valley that stretched north from the rocky First Cataract of the Nile. This Egypt came out of the African world, with its tribal life and priest-kings who brought rain to their people. Upper Egypt always kept in touch with its African neighbors. At the same time, the people of Upper Egypt had been forced to cooperate to survive on their narrow farmlands. As a result, they developed politically sooner than did Lower Egypt.

Lower Egypt was the broad Delta where the Nile split into many rivulets. Here were more fertile lands, marshes of reed and papyrus, lush pastures, and a rich stock of wildlife. The towns were more spread out and there was less need for the people to cooperate. Moreover, Lower Egypt had some contact with the outside world—the eastern Mediterranean, Libya to the west, and the lands to the north and east where many Semitic people lived. Thus the people of Lower Egypt became more advanced culturally than their relatives to the south.

Upper and Lower Egypt were divided in still other ways. They spoke many different dialects and worshiped many different gods. It might seem, then, that they could never be united, but they had a bond that proved to be stronger than all the forces that pulled them apart. The bond was the Nile River—the god "who comes to nourish Egypt." It gave Egypt a unity that most lands of the time would never know.

In Mesopotamia, for instance, the city-states shared a common background. But they were spread out with no clear center, and there was continual rivalry among them. Furthermore, Mesopotamia was surrounded by many other lands and was always in contact with foreign peoples and forces. Egypt, confined to the Nile valley, drew strength from its isolation. From the beginning, too, the Egyptians looked to a central authority in the person of the king worshiped as a god. Despite all their differences, the people, the regions, the kings, and the gods were held together by the Nile.

A UNITED EGYPT

For some time before they actually united, however, the kings of the north and south fought to control more of each other's villages and farmlands along the Nile. Then, about 3200 B.C., King Narmer of Upper Egypt made a bold move. Capturing only the main towns and large estates along the way, he went up into the Delta and took the capital of Lower Egypt. The few nobles and chieftains who resisted were beheaded. Narmer could now wear the red crown of Lower Egypt as well as the white crown of Upper Egypt. As King of the Two Lands he started a new capital at Memphis and set about to bring some unity to the villages strung along the Nile.

Narmer could do little in his lifetime, but dur-

C. WOOD SCULPTURE, PANEL, 2500 B.C.

ing the next few centuries other kings made a true nation out of the Two Lands. There were still many gods—for every city and craft, for everything that men did and everything in nature—but certain gods such as Horus came to be recognized by everyone. The country was divided into districts, each governed by a man appointed by the king. They saw to it that taxes were collected and that the fields were drained and irrigated. For the purpose of keeping records, a special calendar with a 365-day year was adopted, as were standard measures for surveying fields and dividing produce.

HIEROGLYPHS AND PAPYRUS

Although the Egyptians were somewhat isolated from the rest of the world, they could hardly help but be influenced by their neighbors in Mesopotamia. But the Egyptians gave their own stamp to everything they adopted. For example, the Mesopotamians had developed writing, in which each sign stood for a syllable. The Egyptians borrowed the idea but made their own set of signs from familiar objects, most of which also stood for sounds. Thus, when they wanted to write King Narmer's name, they placed a small fish called a "nar" over a chisel, pronounced "mer." This gave them "Narmer."

Using these picture-signs, or hieroglyphs, the Egyptians began to carve and paint inscriptions on

C.

their monuments. The scribes who wrote the letters and kept the records developed a quicker way of writing. They used a reed pen and ink to write on sheets of papyrus, made of the pressed fibers of papyrus plants. With such materials the scribes found it easy to simplify and round off the little picture signs. It took much training to be able to handle this flowing script, or hieratic writing, and the scribes became a highly respected class.

"A CITY FOR THE DEAD"

Egypt was now a growing nation. It took control of territory far up the Nile, carried on trade with the Phoenicians along the Mediterranean coast, and began to work the rich copper mines of the Sinai Peninsula. Up and down the Nile sailed many ships, taking government officials to their posts and picking up produce for taxes. On the great estates along the river stood fine houses whose owners had musicians and dancers to entertain them. In the marshes and thickets, men hunted wild birds and game. In the fields and villages, people were sowing and reaping the crops, tending the animals, and celebrating their festivals.

Most of the people worked on their own small farms or on the great estates, and seldom went far from their village. Sometimes, however, the men went off to serve with the army or to work on some royal building project. And if a man showed great skill as a craftsman or sailor, he could hope to be hired by the king. Men with ambition could also become scribes or priests or government officials. The government had become a complicated organization, with all its officials and activities supervised by the vizier, the man "to whom is reported all that is and is not." Each day the vizier, in turn, reported on the state of affairs to the king and received new orders.

Over all Egyptians, like the top stone of a pyramid, was the king. He assured harmony to the nation, fertility to the land, and the blessings of the gods to his people. They felt that when the king prospered, Egypt prospered; in working for him they were working for their own well-being. The king was worshiped as a god. Sculptors depicted him towering over all other men or sitting in eter-

RARE SPICES, PLANTS, ANIMALS, GOLD, AND INCENSE WERE BROUGHT TO EGYPT FROM THE COUNTRIES OF THE MIDDLE EAST.

nal majesty. Later the king was called the Pharaoh, the "great house" who sheltered all his people. The high nobles and officials wanted to be buried near him, for the king would have eternal life and they wanted to share it.

For some time the kings had been building larger and larger tombs. They were mudbrick structures, with sloping sides and flat tops. Then, about 2700 B.C., King Djoser decided that he would have a special tomb. He consulted his vizier, Imhotep, a brilliant man who was a doctor and writer as well as an engineer. Together they planned a tomb that would dwarf the ones that had been built at Saqqara, outside Memphis.

Imhotep supervised the construction of a series of terraces rising to form a step-like pyramid. It was made of stone; in fact, it was the largest stone structure of its day. Within the pyramid was the burial chamber for King Djoser, and around it were temples and a great wall. It was truly a city for the dead, and everyone who saw it was convinced that the Pharaoh was a god.

THE GREAT PYRAMIDS

A century later, King Khufu decided that he must have a tomb to surpass all others. He chose a site at Giza, and with his Vizier, Hemon, he planned a structure that could be enlarged as his reign went on. It was an enormous job of organization to supply the men and materials that were needed. Hundreds of stonecutters were put to work in quarries to cut the great rough blocks of limestone. At Giza, a village grew up to house the thousands of men who worked there, and arrange-

MEN FROM ALL PARTS OF THE EGYPTIAN EMPIRE, MANY OF THEM SKILLED ARTISANS, WERE PUT TO WORK ON VARIOUS PROJECTS, HERE CONSTRUCTING A SMALL BOAT.

ments were made to feed them. The heavy blocks of stone, some weighing as much as 15 tons, were hauled in during the flood season, when thousands of extra workers were employed.

After enough blocks had reached Giza for work to begin, the base of the pyramid was laid. Then, starting at each corner, ramps of rubble and mud were built. The second layer of blocks was dragged up the ramps and placed in position on the base. As the pyramid rose, layer by layer, the ramps rose alongside. Several thousand men dragged the blocks on sledges up three of the ramps; other men dragged the empty sledges down the fourth ramp.

The rough limestone for the center of the pyramid was quarried nearby, but the finer stone for the outer casing came from across the river and had to be floated over on barges. The final trimming and polishing of the stones was done at the pyramid by skilled masons, who worked with great precision. Blocks weighing two and a half tons were cut so that their edges and corners fit almost perfectly. Engineers checked to make sure that each layer was flat and square. When the final stone was in place, the men worked down from the top, smoothing the outer blocks and removing the ramps.

Finally, after about twenty years of work, the great, gleaming pyramid rose from the desert. Built of more than two million blocks of limestone, it stood some 480 feet high. Around the pyramid were other structures, such as a great wall, a covered passage to the temple at the river's edge, and the smaller tombs of those privileged to join the king in the afterlife. Later, the great pyramids of Khafre and Menkaure, the kings who followed Khufu, were built nearby.

Within the pyramids and tombs lay the kings, nobles, and high officials in their coffins, their bodies preserved with rare oils and fluids and wrapped in linen. In the burial chambers were the foods, clothing, jewelry, weapons, and everything else they needed in the afterlife. In the temples at the base of the great pyramids, priests performed rites to honor the spirit of the kings.

The pyramids were a ceremonial center from which all Egyptians could draw strength and pride. But the land could not afford many such memorials to the dead kings. Menkaure's pyramid, in fact, was quite a bit smaller than Khufu's and Khafre's, and the kings who followed built still smaller tombs. It was not only that people resented the expense, but also that other groups were now challenging the power of the kings. The priests at Heliopolis, "the city of the sun" where the sun-god Re was worshiped, were growing much stronger. At the same time, district governors and local nobles were beginning to rule their territories more independently.

THE NEW KINGS

By 2200 B.C., Egypt had entered a period of upheaval. Law and order broke down. The tombs were robbed, the stone was stripped from the buildings, and the priests no longer performed the proper ceremonies. Local nobles took up the burial

THOUSANDS OF PERSONS, INCLUDING SLAVES, WORKED ON THE GREAT PYRAMID OF KHUFU.

customs of royalty. "Why, really," wrote one man, "the land spins around as does the potter's wheel. The robber is now the possessor of riches." And another complained, "I show thee the land topsy-turvy. That which never happened has happened."

In spite of the disorder, it looked as though a new kind of society might develop, one in which

THE HYKSOS INVADERS CAME SOUTH FROM SYRIA AND PALESTINE.

more people would share the power. Instead, the old order was restored by force. By 2050 B.C., a family at Thebes, a city on Upper Egypt, had gained command over much of Egypt. They were followed by another family from Thebes, the twelfth great dynasty to rule over the Two Lands. The new kings wisely moved their capital from Thebes to a city nearer the border of Upper and Lower Egypt. They did not try to take away the powers of the local officials and governors, but only asked for their loyalty. In this way the twelfth dynasty was able to rule for two centuries.

Once again, Egypt was prospering. The old boundaries were restored, careful records of the Nile's flood levels were kept, and there was much building. At Harawa a temple was built with so many courtyards and colonnades that it became known as a labyrinth, or maze. Egypt's trading ships once more went far up the Nile. They sailed to Crete, to the ports of Phoenicia, and even to the land of Punt on the African coast. Egypt sent out its gold, metalwork, and papyrus and received in return the wine, oils, and wood of its neighbors.

Since the new kings were from Thebes, they naturally encouraged the worship of the Theban gods. The most important of them was Amon, the invisible god of the air. The Egyptians were used to accepting new gods and soon combined him with the sun-god Re. Amon-Re became the national god of Egypt. The king himself was once again looked upon as a god, and gradually he regained most of his power. Still, the king was no longer the superhuman figure who sat rigid and isolated, as in the days of the old kingdom.

Once again, the Egyptians were self-confident and cheerful, as they had been in the early days.

THEY WERE THE FIRST TO INTRODUCE THE HORSE TO EGYPT.

For, despite the great tombs and the funeral ceremonies, the Egyptians were lovers of life. It was because of their love of life that they were so much concerned with what happened after death. They hated to give up the good things of life and wanted to go on enjoying them in the afterworld.

The mass of poor and illiterate Egyptians were barely affected by the prosperity of the years under the twelfth dynasty. They could only accept their position in society and hope that peace and order were maintained. For the rich and educated, however, life was good. Perhaps this was best expressed by an Egyptian court official named Sinuhe. Even though he had to flee from Egypt because he once offended the ruling powers, he never lost his love for his homeland. Later, when he wrote the story of his life, he expressed his appreciation for having been allowed to return.

Sinuhe's autobiography was only one of many works that made this the golden age of Egyptian literature. Letters, tales, proverbs, religious works —all showed great skill in expression. People wrote with charm and humor, and enjoyed playing with words. The language and manner of writing survived for centuries as the classic Egyptian style.

The good life of the twelfth dynasty could not last. By 1800 B.C., Egypt began to lose some of its influence in Palestine and Syria. In western Asia, people were on the move, and some of the unsettled and migrant peoples began to enter Egypt's Delta. The Egyptians called them the Hyksos, "the rulers of foreign lands." They were a mixed group from western Asia, although most were Semitic tribesmen. Some were harmless shepherds and drifters, but others were armed raiders.

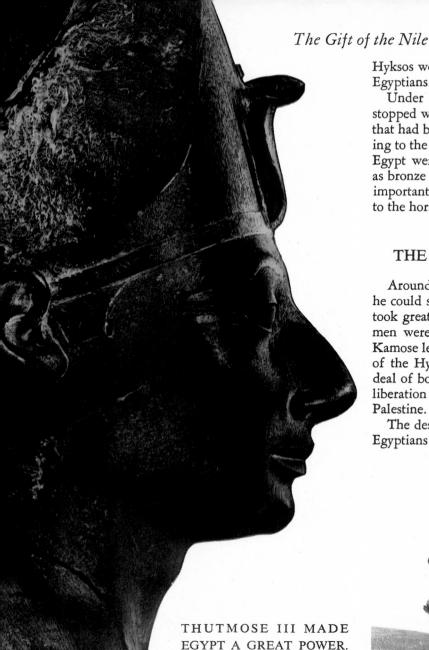

THUTMOSE III MADE
EGYPT A GREAT POWER.

Hyksos were satisfied with tribute from the native Egyptians.

Under the rule of the Hyksos, the Egyptians stopped working at the building and the literature that had been their pride. Such things meant nothing to the Hyksos warriors, whose contributions to Egypt were good body armor and weapons such as bronze swords, and a strong kind of bow. Most important, the Hyksos introduced the Egyptians to the horse and chariot.

THE HYKSOS ARE DEFEATED

Around 1600 B.C., Kamose of Thebes decided he could stand no more and organized a revolt. It took great courage, for many of his own countrymen were satisfied to keep things as they were. Kamose led a fleet down the Nile, wiped out some of the Hyksos strongholds, and captured a great deal of booty. His brother Ahmose completed the liberation and chased the Hyksos all the way into Palestine.

The despised Hyksos were gone at last, and the Egyptians were free to take up their own ways.

A stronger Egypt would soon have dealt with the Hyksos. Instead, by 1730 B.C., the Hyksos were taking power into their own hands.

From their capital in the Delta, the Hyksos moved out and set up several other armed strongholds. Hoping to be accepted by the people, they took Egyptian names, adopted the royal titles and ceremonies, and tried to appear as the official successors of the great kings. They neglected the Egyptian gods and temples, however, and were never really accepted by the people. In the end, the

They hurried to show their gratitude to the gods by building new temples and reviving the old ceremonies. Now that Thebans were ruling again, the Theban god Amon was once more worshiped by the whole nation. The priests who officiated over the cult of Amon began to gain such wealth and power that they would rival the kings and other officials.

But the Hyksos had left a permanent mark on the Egyptians. They had been conquered by foreigners—barbarians who did not even worship the proper gods. While recovering from this great shock, the Egyptians began to show a more ambitious spirit. At first the Theban kings were occupied in putting down revolts among various local nobles; then they began to extend their rule up the Nile into Africa. No longer satisfied with trading, Egypt also began to look abroad for possible conquests.

THE WARRIOR KING

Under Amenhotep I, Thutmose I, and Thutmose II, Egypt became a military power, using the horse and chariot, paid soldiers, and the new weapons and battle tactics. The Pharaohs themselves now led the army into the field, only one of the signs that the times were changing. From 1520–1480 B.C., Egypt was even ruled by a queen, Hatshepsut. She was a forceful personality who built new temples, advanced trade, and brought peace and glory to her people. It was quite different from the old days, when the god-king was far removed from the people and the queen sat silently at his side.

Following her death, Hatshepsut was succeeded by her husband, Thutmose III. Thutmose III was determined to make Egypt into an imperial power. He was especially anxious to control Palestine and Syria, for they were at the crossroads of many trading routes. His chief opponent there was the prince of Kadesh, a city-state on the Orontes River in Syria. The prince organized all the other princes and chieftains of the region and they brought their troops to Megiddo, a city in Palestine that commanded the route to the north. Thutmose III brought his Egyptian army up, and there on the plain of Megiddo they fought a furious battle.

LED BY THUTMOSE III, THE EGYPTIANS ATTACKED THE SYRIANS
IN THE BATTLE OF MEGIDDO.

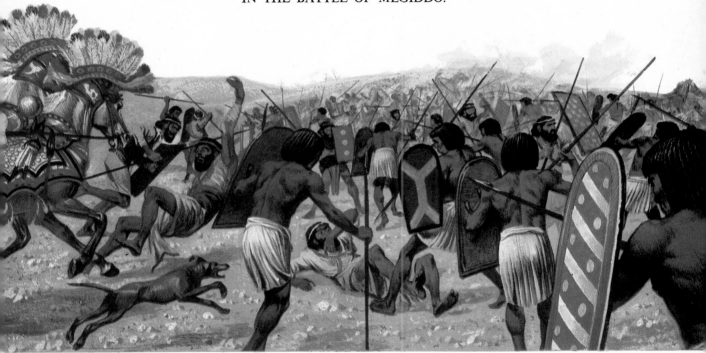

The Egyptians won the battle, but they captured the city only after a siege of many months. Rather than slaughter his enemies, Thutmose III simply demanded that they take an oath of loyalty. Even so, Thutmose III had to fight continuously to hold his empire in western Asia. Throughout all his campaigns, Egypt grew richer. Her ships, caravans, messengers, and armed patrols went everywhere, from Turkey in the north to Nubia in the south. Egypt was truly an international force.

Egypt's empire brought wealth and power, but it also brought responsibilities and still greater changes. Egypt now had to support a large professional army and vast numbers of government officials. Through their contacts with many different foreign peoples, the Egyptians' traditional attitudes were changing. Under the earlier dynasties, art, society, religion, and government had been rigid, but they also gave the people a sense of security. Now it seemed that nothing could be depended on for long.

THE SUN WORSHIPER

About 1370 B.C., Amenhotep IV came to the throne. He had none of the vigorous, out-going manners of the recent Pharaohs. He was not a good athlete and he was no soldier. He was a withdrawn, studious man, with a thin face and sloping shoulders. Even as a boy he had been interested in religion, and as he grew older he became dissatisfied with all the established gods and their priests. Finally Amenhotep IV rejected Amon, Re, and all the other gods and began to worship only Aton, the life-giving sun. Aton was to be the universal god, Amenhotep decided, and there were to be no idols of Aton. He would be shown only as the disk of the sun, with the rays coming down and ending in hands that gave life to all things.

Amenhotep changed his own name to Akhnaton, meaning "to the well-being of Aton." He also decided to move the capital away from Thebes, with its powerful and jealous priesthood of Amon. He wanted to start a completely different way of life, and he chose a new site at Amarna. There he began to build a great religious center, with palaces and temples open to the sun instead of closed and dark like the sanctuaries of the other gods. Aton gave and demanded truth, and everything had to be exposed to view.

AKHNATON AND NEFERTITI RULED FROM THEIR CAPITAL AT AMARNA.

Life at Amarna was different in many ways. Akhnaton and his beautiful wife Nefertiti moved about in public. Their people could see them playing with their six lovely daughters. And when one of the girls died, Akhnaton was not ashamed to show his grief.

Akhnaton encouraged artists to work in the new spirit of truth and openness. Artists in the old kingdom had not tried to show realistic movement or expressions. Servants, children, and workers might be depicted with realistic detail, but the Pharaohs and other important people were shown as ideal beings. Classic Egyptian art tried to freeze action and emotion into something universal and eternal. Under Akhnaton, art became more natural. Akhnaton himself was not depicted as some distant god, but as a relaxed human being. Writers, too, gave a truer picture of the life around them. They began to drop the classic literary language and use the language of their day.

In time, Akhnaton became almost a fanatic about his new faith. He was determined to do away with the other gods, especially Amon, the god from Thebes. Akhnaton sent agents around the land to cut the name "Amon" out of stone inscriptions. He also demanded that his people worship himself as the son of Aton. The Egyptians were accustomed to worshiping their Pharaoh as a god, but they could not understand why Akhnaton rejected their many other gods.

Akhnaton was never able to attract many true believers outside the royal circle. Worse still, he made many enemies throughout Egypt by turning his back on the empire his ancestors had built up. As the Egyptians lost influence in Africa and western Asia, they lost the source of their wealth. In the final years of his reign, Akhnaton became sickly and weak. When he died, his religion died with him, and the Egyptians happily returned to all their old familiar gods.

THE TOMB OF TUTANKHAMON

Akhnaton's successor, Tutankhaton, was only nine years old, and the priests and high officials held the real power. Now that they were free to worship the god Amon again, they changed the young king's name to Tutankhamon. When he suddenly died at the age of 18, the priests and officials were careful to give him the full royal burial. He was placed in three caskets, one within the other, and all richly decorated. These were

THE GODDESS
THOUERIS

placed in a great stone sarcophagus within the burial chamber, and all around were the objects for the afterlife. Amid all the shining gold were two small amulets and a dagger that were probably the most important treasures in the tomb, although no one realized it at the time. They were made of iron, and it was iron that would one day help to bring an end to golden Egypt.

The old gods and the conservative forces were back in power, but they could not revive the classic Egyptian spirit. Narrow laws now replaced broad traditions, magic replaced faith. Then, about 1290 B.C., Ramesses II became king, and it seemed as if he would bring back the old glory. Once again, Egypt was fighting and building. Yet behind much of what Ramesses II did was his desire to show off. Although he was unable to defeat the Hittites decisively, he boasted of his great victory at Kadesh, in Syria, and had the story carved on several monuments. And the monuments he built, such as the temple cut into the cliff at Abu Simbel, were often monstrously large.

Ramesses II had more than 100 children and ruled for more than sixty years, yet he left no foundation for Egypt's future. Throughout Asia and the Mediterranean, whole peoples were on the move, and among them were the Philistines. The Egyptians were able to keep the Philistines out of Egypt, but they themselves lost influence in Palestine and the Phoenician ports.

THE END OF THE PHARAOHS

The great days of Egypt were over. One reason was that iron was coming into use among the peoples of western Asia and the eastern Mediterranean. Egypt had no deposits of iron ore. To keep up with other countries and make the new and stronger weapons and tools, it had to import iron. This put an extra strain on its economy. Prices rose, wages fell, and the great tombs were continually robbed for their treasures. By 1100 B.C., Egypt was a divided land. A Pharaoh still sat on the throne, but merchants, priests, and the army held the real power.

It was a difficult time, and many Egyptians tried to find comfort in the cult of the dead presided over by the god Osiris. Various groups of foreigners had been coming into Egypt for some time, and now they became more and more powerful. By 950 B.C., a Libyan had established a new dy-

A PROCESSION AT THE TEMPLE AT KARNAK, WHICH WAS DEDICATED TO THE GOD AMON

nasty of kings. About 720 B.C., an Ethiopian made the first successful invasion of Egypt in a thousand years and took over the throne.

Then, by 525 B.C., Persia easily conquered

48

Egypt and turned it into a province of its empire. Later, Alexander the Great claimed Egypt for his own, and still later the Roman emperors did the same. The great Pharaohs, the power, the wealth, and the glory were gone. All that the Egyptians could rely on was the Nile, the mighty river that rose and fell each year as always, bringing fertile soil to their farmlands.

49

The People of One God

3000 B.C.-30 B.C.

ON the plains of Mesopotamia, a young man stood gazing up at the stars that glittered from the dark sky of night. He was Abraham, a native of the Sumerian city of Ur. Abraham was a Hebrew, one of the many tribes of Semites said to have been descended from Shem, the son of Noah who had been saved from a great flood many years before. Like all people of his time, Abraham believed in many gods throughout nature. But as he studied the pattern of the stars for the gods' message, Abraham began to feel he was in the presence of a Lord God who was above all the other gods with their idols and temples and sacrifices. Abraham felt, too, that this Lord God would take special care of those who lived up to his demands.

Abraham became so devoted to this idea that years later he was inspired to leave Mesopotamia and start a new nation whose people would worship only the Lord God. With his family and tents and flocks, he made his way westward to the land of Canaan. After many setbacks, Abraham died there, content to know that his son Isaac would carry on the family. Isaac prospered and was

followed by his son Jacob, whose life was such a struggle that he was honored with the name Israel, meaning "struggler with God." Jacob had twelve sons, each of whom founded a tribe, and they and all their descendants became known as Israelites. One of Jacob's sons, Joseph, became an important official in the Egyptian court, and when a famine in the land of Canaan threatened to wipe out the Hebrews, they all joined Joseph in Egypt.

This was the story told in the Bible and the traditions of the people who honored Abraham, Isaac, and Jacob as their patriarchs, or the founding fathers of their people and religion. Long before the stories were written down, they were passed·on from generation to generation, and many details were added. Still, the stories kept alive the basic truth of this people's past. Since at least 3000 B.C., nomadic Semite tribes had been moving out of the Arabian deserts to settle in more prosperous lands. Each tribe was headed by one man, usually the oldest in the tribe; each tribe worshiped many gods, but had one particular god who especially looked after its people. Among

50

THE SONS OF ABRAHAM MADE A LONG
JOURNEY INTO THE LAND OF CANAAN.

these tribes were the Hebrews, and about 1650
B.C. the ones known as Israelites seem to have settled in the land of Goshen, in the eastern part of
the Nile Delta.

On Egypt's fertile meadows, the Israelites and
their flocks grew in numbers. Not all the Israelites
kept up their faith in the Lord God of the patriarchs, but they stayed together as a people and
enjoyed some freedom. Then new Pharaohs came
to the throne and the Israelites were forced into
slavery. Instead of tending their flocks, they had to
work in the fields or on the Pharaoh's great building projects. The Israelites were broken in spirit
and Abraham's vision of a nation under the Lord
God seemed to be ended.

One day, some of the Israelite slaves were at
work when an Egyptian began to beat one of them.
As it happened, a man by the name of Moses was
passing by at that moment. Although of Hebrew
descent, Moses had been raised in the Egyptian
court and he had never been sure of his feelings
about the Israelites. Now he leaped forward and
killed the Egyptian. From that time on, Moses was
to live as an Israelite. At first he had to flee Egypt,
and he spent some time with a Semitic tribe, whose
god Yahweh aroused his faith. Moses then returned to Egypt and, after many difficulties, led
the Israelites out of Egypt.

THE EXODUS FROM EGYPT

Their plan was to make their way to Canaan,
the land of Abraham, Isaac, and Jacob. While
crossing the Sinai Peninsula, the Israelites became
discouraged, but Moses did not lose faith. He led
them to Mount Sinai, and there they accepted
Yahweh, the god he had come to know in exile,
as their own. Yahweh, Moses assured them, was
the Lord God of the patriarchs and would treasure
the Israelites above all other people.

In return, however, the Israelites had to enter
into an agreement, called a covenant. They had
to agree to obey certain basic laws, which later
became known as the Ten Commandments.
Among them were laws that said the Israelites
should worship their Lord God above all other
gods; they should not make any idols to worship;
they should not take an oath in the name of the

Lord God unless they honestly meant it; they
should observe the Sabbath as a day of rest; they
should honor their parents; they should not kill
anyone; they should not steal; they should not lie
about their neighbors; and they should not be en-
vious of their neighbors' possessions.

Many other peoples of that time had laws, but
there was something quite different about the laws
the Israelites were asked to accept. Most laws up to
that time were concerned largely with keeping order in society. Furthermore, they were based on
the power of rulers, who themselves were above
the laws. But now, for the first time, there were
laws that applied to rulers as well as to everyone
else. For the first time, too, laws were based on
religious ideals. The laws of the Israelites con-
nected men's relations with all other men to men's
devotion to a god.

THE LAND OF CANAAN

Such an idea was new, and it was not easy for
the Israelites to live up to it. At the same time, they
suffered great hardships as they made their way
to Canaan. For many years, led by Moses, they
wandered in the wilderness of the Sinai Peninsula. During these years their religion began to
develop, so that when they finally reached Canaan
they were more secure in their faith. Moses himself
died just as they were about to enter Canaan.

It was a bad time for the Israelites to be with-
out a leader, for the territory they considered their
promised land was already inhabited by many
people. It was only a small area, from the Mediterranean Sea to the Jordan River and the Dead
Sea, and in many ways it was an uninviting land,
with barren mountain ridges and hot, dry low-
lands. Even so, Semitic tribes had been migrating
there for many hundreds of years and they had
managed to make a good life for themselves with
their farms and flocks.

Chief among the settled peoples were the Canaanites, who gave their name to the land. They
had built up many towns and fortified cities, and
the Canaanites along the coast, known as Phoenicians, had rich trading ports. There were many
other tribes in and around the land of Canaan, and
some of them were close relatives of the Israelites,
but none of them welcomed the new settlers.

Fortunately, the Israelites found a new leader in
Joshua, who was not only a student of Moses but a
good soldier as well. After they had crossed the

A STONE CARVING OF A KING OF ISRAEL
(1000-850 B.C.)

Jordan River into Canaan, Joshua led the Israelites to their first victory against the strongly fortified city of Jericho. This gave the Israelites courage, and they moved on to conquer other cities and tribes. Many years of fighting, however, lay before them.

As they began to settle on the land, the Israelites became separated and their dream of a nation began to fade. They adopted the ways of the Canaanites, who were a much more advanced people and had tools, weapons, metal, pottery, and drainage systems. The Canaanites even had a new way of writing, using a few signs to indicate all sounds, and the Israelites began to use this script as their alphabet. Some of the Israelites even turned away from Yahweh and worshiped the gods of the Canaanites.

Meanwhile, Joshua had died, and no single strong leader came forward to hold the scattered tribes together. New leaders arose in various tribes, however, usually by commanding the tribe in its fights with its enemies. Because they were allowed to sit in judgment over their people and settle disputes within the tribe, these men were called judges. For many years the Israelites depended on the judges to lead them in their struggle to survive in Canaan.

Their worst enemy was now the Philistines, a non-Semitic people from the eastern Mediterranean who had settled on the coastal plain between Egypt and the Phoenician ports. The disorganized peoples of Canaan were no match for the Philistine warriors, who had iron weapons and disciplined battle tactics. One of the tribal judges, Samson, had some success against them, but he was captured and killed. The Philistines came to control so much of the land of Canaan that it was known as Palestine.

The Israelites were desperate for a leader. They thought of choosing Samuel, a wise man respected by all the people, but he could not lead them into battle. Samuel said, rather, that they must give up worshiping the Canaanite gods and renew their faith in Yahweh, the Lord God of the patriarchs. Samuel's teachings brought some unity to the Israelites, but they still insisted they needed a strong ruler. Just then, as it happened, a brave farmer named Saul led his tribe to victory over some neighboring raiders. This was what the Israelites needed to revive their courage, and they appointed Saul king over all the tribes. At last the Israelites felt they were on their way to becoming a nation.

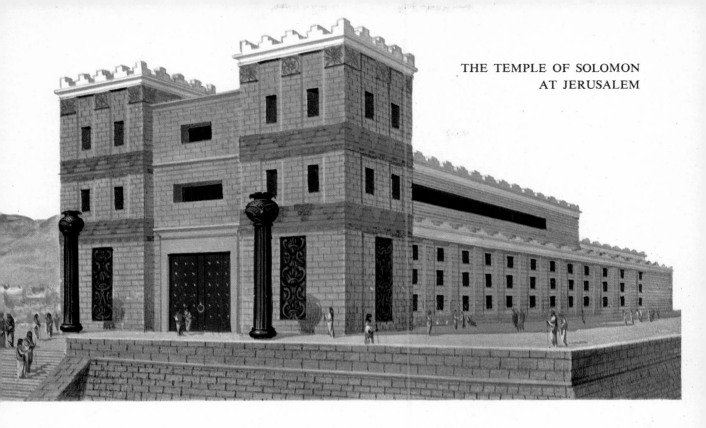

Using guerrilla tactics, Saul led the fight against the Philistines. As the Philistines began to retreat, the Israelites rallied around Saul, and yet they were not completely satisfied with him. He was a rough, simple man, who held his council meetings under a tree in a field. And, as he won more victories, he became proud. He was a moody man, too, unpredictable in his actions, and the Israelites began to wonder if they had made the right choice.

THE GLORY OF SOLOMON

One of Saul's attendants in camp at this time was a young man named David. David was a handsome, gracious youth, and after proving himself in battle against the Philistines he became popular with all the Israelites. Saul was so crazed with jealousy that David had to flee and live with the people in the distant hills. After Saul died, David became known as a warrior and, in time, all the tribes recognized him as king. David came from the tribe of Judah, whose members were called Jews. They became so powerful that later all the Israelites were known by this name.

David chose Jerusalem as a new capital, and there he built great walls and a palace. He led his people in driving out the Philistines for the last time, and he made the borders safe against neighboring tribes and foreign powers. He reorganized the priesthood, the army, and the civil service, and established the Israelites' first truly national government.

David himself was an unusual man. He could fight and kill his enemies, yet he was a fine musician and poet. He was often selfish, yet in the end he knew he was bound by the laws of his people and their agreement with the Lord God Yahweh. As he grew older, he became more gentle and humble. His greatest sorrow came when his son Absalom led a revolt against him and was killed in battle. The only satisfaction left for David was to see another son, Solomon, named as heir to the throne.

Solomon was no warrior like his father, nor did he have any of David's simple ways. Solomon built up the kingdom by trade and diplomacy. He brought peace to his people and became known far beyond the borders of his small kingdom. The Israelites, however, knew that there was another side to Solomon's glory. It was true that he made his land prosper, but much of the wealth went to satisfy Solomon's own vanity and ambitions. He strengthened the government, but he did away with many of the traditional rights of the tribes. And although he built a magnificent temple to the Lord God Yahweh in Jerusalem, Solomon himself turned to worshiping foreign idols.

The Israelites felt that Solomon was a wise man but that he lived foolishly. They began to grow restless, objecting to the high taxes and to the forced labor of his building projects. The tribes in the north were especially resentful, for they felt no strong attachment to the royal house of Judah. When Solomon died, they demanded certain rights from Solomon's son. He refused them, and so, about 930 B.C., ten tribes in the north revolted against the Kingdom of Judah and set up their own Kingdom of Israel.

Once more the Israelites' dream of a kingdom under the Lord God Yahweh was shattered. The two kingdoms began to fight their neighbors and each other, and the people even fought among themselves. In the northern Kingdom of Israel, there were assassinations and plots to seize the throne. In two centuries, Israel had nineteen kings. At times, Israel seemed to be prospering, and often it held power over the Kingdom of Judah. But it was not real power, for the existence of the Kingdom of Israel depended on the truly great powers, such as Egypt and Assyria. By 715 B.C., the Assyrians had completely conquered the Kingdom of Israel. Its ten tribes were led away to be resettled and became lost in the great deserts and cities of the Near East. The Kingdom of Judah survived, but only by paying tribute to the Assyrians.

THE BABYLONIAN CAPTIVITY

During the five centuries the Israelites had been in Canaan, it often seemed that they had forgotten the teachings of Moses. Yet all this time there were men who reminded them of their duty to the Lord God Yahweh and to each other. These men were the *nebiim,* the spokesmen of God—the prophets. These prophets did not try to predict the future. Instead, they criticized the way the Israelites behaved in the present. When the prophets spoke of the future, it was to warn the Israelites that their troubles would continue until they returned to the faith of the patriarchs.

Century after century, the prophets spoke out, never fearing the rich or the mighty. Nathan, Elijah, Amos, Hosea, Isaiah, Micah, Jeremiah—some were educated and respected men, some were plain men of the hills. But whether they spoke with great style or in simple words, with bitterness or with tenderness, the prophets tried to make the Israelites renew their agreement with the Lord God Yahweh. "Let justice roll down as the waters, and righteousness as a mighty stream," cried one prophet. "Woe, for the end of my people, Israel, is at hand. I can no longer forgive," warned another. "It hath been shown thee, O man, what is good, and what Yahweh doth demand of thee: only to do justice and to love mercy and to walk humbly with thy God," said still another.

Although they never stopped reminding the Israelites of their covenant with the Lord, the prophets carried the idea of the law far beyond anything foreseen by Moses. Indeed, the prophets put forth ideas of justice and responsibility to all men that were beyond anything conceived of by any people of that time. Here again the Israelites were introducing something new, an idea that came to be called social justice. In some of the prophets' teachings, moreover, the Yahweh of the Israelite tribes became the Lord God of all men. In the centuries to come, men of many faiths would find inspiration in the words of the prophets.

At the time when the prophets spoke out, however, most of the Israelites paid no attention until it was too late. The Babylonians had taken over the Assyrian Empire, and in 597 B.C. the dreaded King Nebuchadnezzar of Babylon captured Jerusalem and took the king and his leading citizens back to Babylon as prisoners. The Jews who remained in the Kingdom of Judah later revolted, but the Babylonians returned in 586 B.C. This time Jerusalem was destroyed, and many more Jews were led off to Babylon. The Israelites were now scattered all over the Near East. The temple and the nation of Abraham and Moses were in ruins.

To the Jews captive in Babylon, it seemed that the prophets had been right. The Israelites were being punished for breaking their agreement with their Lord God Yahweh. In their despair, they began to revive their old faith and traditional ways. They also started some new practices that were to have a great effect on other religions as well as their own.

For one thing, their religion had come to be bound up with the great temple at Jerusalem, with its ceremonies and its powerful priests. In Babylon, where there was no temple, the Israelites gathered in meeting houses to pray and tell stories of their past. Out of this was to come the synagogue, and the idea that religious services could be held wherever a congregation of the faithful gathered. Scribes, priests, and students collected

The People of One God

and wrote down the history, laws, and stories on scrolls. From this would grow a respect for learning and for the wise teachers, or rabbis.

Perhaps most important, the Jews in Babylon came to realize that their Lord God Yahweh could exist away from the temple and outside their land. The Lord God, in other words, was not restricted to any one place or to any one people. This discovery was the greatest contribution of the ancient Jews to religious thought. Later it would be called monotheism, "the idea of one god." But monotheism meant more than just worshiping one god. It meant that the Lord God was within all men and above all creation. Beyond this, the Jews believed that the way to serve the Lord God was to serve all their fellow men.

For all its hardships, the Babylonian captivity left the Jews a much stronger people. Their faith was rewarded when Cyrus of Persia conquered Babylon in 538 B.C. and gave the Jews their freedom. Not all of them wanted to leave, but a small group set out carrying some of the treasures of the temple their parents had brought with them some forty years before. After a journey of several weeks, they arrived in Jerusalem, only to find ruins and weeds. For many years they could barely survive, but finally they rebuilt their temple.

Those who still remembered the great temple of Solomon wept because it was so small and plain, but others saw the temple as the seed of a new Jerusalem.

THE TORAH

The Kingdom of Judah at this time was less than 200 square miles in area, and the small colony of Jews was often defenseless against the many hostile tribes around them. As it happened, a high official at the court of the Persian Emperor was a Jew, Nehemiah. He heard of the Jews' difficulties and got permission to go to Jerusalem to help them. Soon Nehemiah had the Jews rebuilding the walls and defending themselves, and when he saw that they were settled he began to encourage them to live according to the teachings of Moses.

Nehemiah was aided in his reforms by Ezra, a scribe and scholar who had recently arrived from Mesopotamia with a band of Jews sent to colonize the new Kingdom of Judah. Ezra gathered together all the learned men familiar with the history, religion, and laws of the Jews. Working under Ezra, they collected the writings and traditions that had been handed down since the time of the

THE GREAT CITIES OF THE MIDDLE EAST BEFORE THE TIME OF CHRIST

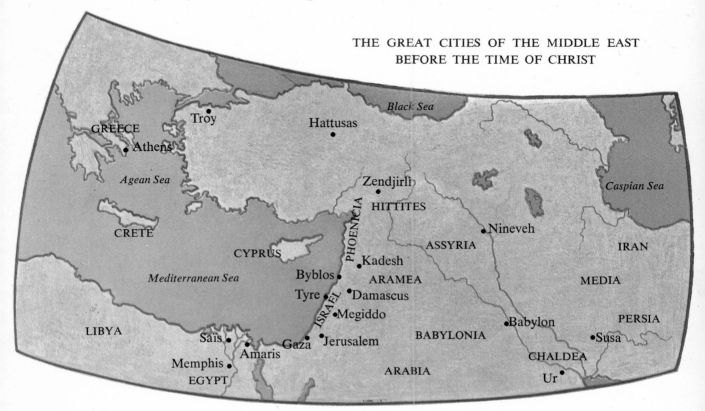

patriarchs and Moses. These were written down in five books, the Pentateuch that made up the first five books of the Bible. In a special ceremony, Ezra read them to the people. Now the Jews had their Torah, or law, which they promised to study and live up to.

As the years passed, other sacred writings were added to the first five books. All together, they made up the Torah that kept the Jewish religion and community alive in Palestine. Palestine itself remained a minor province of the Persian Empire until 323 B.C., when Alexander the Great took control of that empire. For the first time, the Jews found themselves facing the world to their west, and they became caught up in the conflicts of the Greeks and Romans. New masters appeared in Palestine, and the Jews themselves once again became scattered in many different lands.

Throughout all this, the Jews kept their respect for the Torah and their faith in the covenant with God. Such beliefs would help the Jews to survive as a people long after the empires of the ancient world had disappeared. Out of their teachings, moreover, were to come two religions, Christianity and Islam, which would have a still further influence on the world.

The Rise of the Assyrians
1600 B.C.-539 B.C.

DURING the centuries after the Hittites had raided Babylon and rose to power in Turkey and Syria, Mesopotamia was a divided, unproductive land. In the south, Babylonia fell under the rule of foreigners, first the Kassites from the northeast and then the Elamites from the southeast. Neither of these people seemed able to make any advances in civilization. Northern Mesopotamia came under the Mitanni kingdom, which at least introduced trained horses and chariots to the Near East. By the time the native Babylonians regained control and the Mitanni kingdom fell, another people was disturbing the land—the Assyrians.

The Assyrians, who spoke and wrote Akkadian, were close relatives of the Babylonians and had

ASSYRIAN WARRIORS BATTLING NOMADS

played a minor part in Mesopotamian affairs for some time. They made their home in the upper reaches of the Tigris River, where once had been some of the earliest farming communities in the world. The region later came under the influence of various early Sumerian and Babylonian kingdoms to the south. By about 2000 B.C., the Assyrians themselves became independent enough to carry on a thriving trade with people in Turkey. But around 1800 B.C. the Hittites put an end to that, and then the Mitanni kingdom set itself over Assyria.

THE WARRIOR KINGS

Centuries passed, and the Assyrians overthrew a weakened Mitanni kingdom, but even before this they were struggling with Babylonia for control of Mesopotamia. Year after year, lands, cities, trading routes, and outposts changed hands, until the Assyrians gradually won out. By 1100 B.C., under their king Tiglath-Pileser I, the Assyrians were strong enough to begin expanding. Fighting off enemies on all sides, Assyria began to dominate the metal trade with the north and the commercial centers of the Syrian coast. Loot and

(LEFT) ASHURBANIPAL II

tribute made Ashur, the capital of Assyria, a prosperous city. The Assyrians had started on their road of conquest.

During the next five centuries, Assyria became the terror of western Asia. Generation after generation, Assyria produced its warrior kings— Adad-nirari, Ashur-nasir-pal, Shalmaneser, Sennacherib, Esarhaddon, Ashurbanipal. Year after year, these bold men led the Assyrian forces out on campaign. Sometimes they attacked with thousands of foot soldiers, sometimes with groups of charioteers. There were units of horse cavalry, archers, camel troops. But wherever they fought, the Assyrian forces brought death and destruction. They ambushed nomadic tribes, raided outposts, and charged massed armies. All warfare of that time was cruel and bloody, but the Assyrians became known as especially savage fighters. They cut limbs off the dead to steal rings and bracelets, and one Assyrian king claimed the right "to tear out the eyes of the conquered king."

The Assyrians were expert at besieging cities. When a city was captured, it was looted by the troops. Often its citizens were resettled in distant territories or cities. All cities under Assyrian control paid heavy taxes and tribute. Sometimes the conquered people rebelled, but the Assyrian armies always returned. Punishment for the rebel leaders was especially hard. It was not unusual for the Assyrians to strip off a man's skin and hang it on the palace walls.

As the Assyrians expanded their empire, they had to fight off all the neighboring peoples. The Aramaeans from the western deserts, the Urartu tribesmen in the northeast, and the Elamites in the southeast were all a constant threat. Later, tribesmen from the mountains and steppes to the northeast—Cimmerians, Scythians, and Medes—made raids on Assyrian cities and trade routes. It was impossible for the Assyrians to guard all their borders. At their height, the Assyrians had an empire from the Persian Gulf to the borders of Egypt, up the Mediterranean coast, into Turkey, and down the Zagros Mountains, with Mesopotamia at its center. At times they even controlled much of Egypt and part of Armenia.

THE WONDERS OF BABYLON

Although they could be savage fighters, the Assyrians ran their empire well. It was divided into provinces, which were administered by men sent out from the capital. Subject peoples had some self-rule if they paid their taxes and did not rebel, but the Assyrians kept firm control of all their affairs. A network of roads linked the main cities, and messengers on horseback carried the official communications. Troops were stationed everywhere to keep order and to guard trade routes.

From their vast empire, the Assyrians drew in loot and slaves, tribute and taxes. Trade brought in the products of foreign lands—iron from the Turkish hill country, cedar from Lebanon. The Assyrians recruited skilled craftsmen from all nations to work for them. With such wealth and resources at their disposal, the Assyrians built new cities and enlarged old ones. Irrigation systems, grain stores, harbors, temples, palaces, city walls —all were constructed on a scale unknown before.

The average Assyrian shared in such wealth only indirectly; he lived in a simple house and had few possessions. His life was one of hard work, organized around his religion with its many duties and festivals. But every Assyrian could take pleasure in the great cities and their palaces. Ashur and then Kalhu had been fine capitals, but about 710 B.C. Sargon II decided to establish a new one at Khorsabad. He built great brick walls and gateways, with mammoth figures carved in stone. The palace walls were covered with carvings depicting battles, hunting scenes, and ceremonies.

When Sargon's son, Sennacherib, came to the throne, he built still another capital, at Nineveh.

Streets, squares, and flood walls were laid out. The palace was ornamented with rare stones, metals, and woods, the walls decorated with glazed bricks and tapestries. Winged lions and bulls in bronze stood on guard. Around the palace were parks and gardens, with plants and animals imported from distant lands. Miles of canals and an aqueduct 300 yards long brought water into the city.

Sennacherib boasted of this luxurious city: "I had a canal cut into the meadow-lands of Nineveh. I caused a bridge of limestone blocks to span deep ravines, and let those waters pass over it." Yet this same Sennacherib also boasted of destroying Babylon after it had revolted: "The city and its houses, from its foundation to its top, I destroyed, I devastated, I burned with fire. Through the midst of that city I dug canals, I flooded its site with water."

Sennacherib had a library at Nineveh, but it was his grandson Ashurbanipal who set about to make an even more magnificent collection of texts. A staff of scribes was kept busy copying all known texts onto clay tablets—centuries-old Sumerian, Akkadian, and Babylonian texts, as well as more recent Assyrian ones. The library included thousands of tablets, with histories of the various kings and their conquests, collections of hymns and prayers, descriptions of rituals and ceremonies, records of magic, medicine, and astrology, and old tales, such as the story of Gilgamesh.

Yet Ashurbanipal thought nothing of riding forth to battle and capturing and plundering a great city like Thebes, in Egypt. And, after taking Susa, the Elamites' capital, he said: "The graves of the earlier and later kings I destroyed, I devastated, I exposed to the sun. Their bones I carried off to Assyria. I laid restlessness upon their spirits. I deprived them of food offerings and libations of water." Ashurbanipal had captive princes drag his chariot as he went up into the temple to thank his gods, and once he kept a captive on a leash in a kennel.

Most of the people in Ashurbanipal's empire could hardly know or care about his great library. Many of them were only concerned about whether they might be uprooted from their homes and taken to distant parts. Once, some of his subjects had to eat human flesh to keep from starving. A typical prayer of the time was: "The god, known or unknown, has oppressed me. The goddess, known or unknown, has placed suffering upon me. Although I am constantly looking for help, no one takes me by the hand. When I weep, they do not come to my side." The people of Mesopotamia could never

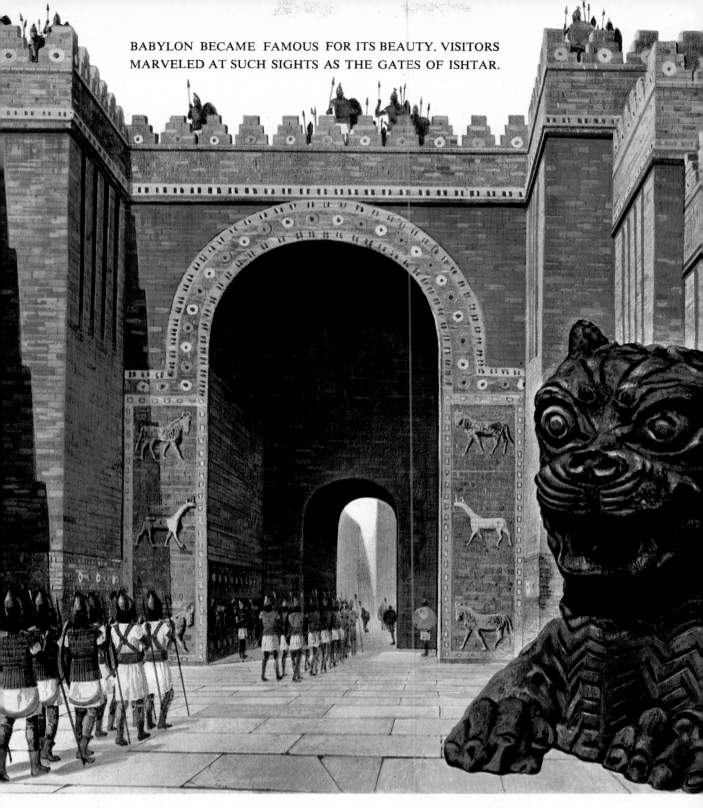

BABYLON BECAME FAMOUS FOR ITS BEAUTY. VISITORS MARVELED AT SUCH SIGHTS AS THE GATES OF ISHTAR.

forget that floods or wars might sweep away all of man's works, even great cities and palaces.

Indeed, the Assyrian empire itself was now threatened, not by foreign invaders, but by people already within its borders. For some centuries,

Babylonia had been falling under the influence of the Chaldaeans, who had originally migrated there from the lands to the west. Again and again the Assyrians sent armies to put down the rebellious Chaldaeans, but the Chaldaeans continued to make trouble. Finally the people of Babylonia themselves rose up in revolt, and in 612 B.C. they captured and burnt Nineveh.

The Babylonians now controlled the empire, and when King Nebuchadnezzar came to the throne he made them a power to be feared and respected. At times he acted like a statesman, but he could be as ruthless as any Assyrian tyrant. He destroyed the city of Jerusalem and took the Jews captive to Babylon.

After the reign of Hammurabi, about 1750 B.C., Babylon had ceased to be a political or commercial center. It continued to be a religious center, however, and its patron god, Marduk, was worshiped throughout Mesopotamia. Under Nebuchadnezzar, Babylon became famous for luxury and sinful living. There were continual festivals and celebrations. Caravans brought rare and exotic products to be sold in its shops. The streets were crowded with soldiers in chariots, pickpockets, fortunetellers, moneylenders, wine merchants, and strolling musicians.

Visitors came from everywhere to see Babylon's beauty and splendor. The great fortified walls were wide enough for two chariots to pass along the top causeway. Great gates and avenues led into the city, with its palaces and temples. The gate and processional way dedicated to the goddess Ishtar had walls lined with animals formed from glazed bricks.

Foreigners were especially impressed with the gardens built on high terraces and watered by an elaborate system of canals. To anyone approaching the city, the gardens appeared to be hanging in mid-air. Visitors also marveled at the great ziggurat, the platform that rose stage by stage with a temple at the top; it seemed as if it reached into the heavens. To the Jews held captive there, however, this "tower of Babel" was only a reminder of the foreign ways that surrounded them.

As a center of wealth and trade, Babylon, attracted men who had special skills or learning. Among them were craftsmen who knew the secrets of tanning leather, making soaps, dyeing cloth, working metals, and making glass. There were also doctors, who had inherited the age-old medical traditions of Mesopotamia. They had many medicines and drugs and could even perform operations. Since everyone, including the craftsmen and doctors, believed that the gods were responsible for everything, each process had to be accompanied by the proper prayers and ceremonies.

THE MEDES AND THE PERSIANS

The most respected men of Babylonia were those who understood the workings of the heavens. For thousands of years, the peoples of Mesopotamia had looked to the skies for signs of what was to happen. Flashing meteors, eclipses, the changing moon, the rising and setting of planets—all were part of the gods' plans and affected men's lives. Priests and wisemen and astrologers believed they could read these signs and foresee famines, floods, and wars, or choose the proper day for any activity. Long ago, too, they had worked out a calendar based on the moon. It had twelve months, with an extra month added every few years.

All this had been passed on through the centuries by traditions and writings. But by the time of Nebuchadnezzar, the sky-watchers had recorded so many observations that they could begin to predict the movements of the heavenly bodies. Later they began to make maps of the sky that showed the positions of the planets and the phases of the

DETAIL OF PERSIAN BRONZE GATES (858-824 B.C.)

moon. This knowledge was only a servant of religion, but later it would provide a basis for the science of astronomy.

But all the learning and wealth of Babylon failed to save it. Nebuchadnezzar built temples throughout his kingdom to honor the gods and also had himself worshiped as a god. Even so, he became troubled in his mind and finally went mad. It was said that he ended his days eating grass like an animal.

Shortly after Nebuchadnezzar died, the gods seemed to desert Babylonia. Cities rebelled, crops failed, prices rose, trade slowed. Then, from the mountains to the northeast, came the old enemies of Mesopotamia, the Medes. Now the Medes were united with other tribesmen, the Persians. In 539 B.C., Babylon was captured by the combined forces of Medes and Persians. For many years, Babylon remained a fine city and the Babylonians were respected for their learning and skills, but Mesopotamia was now ruled by new peoples who worshiped new gods.

A New People, a New Faith

650 B.C. - 330 B.C.

BABYLON, the final capital of Mesopotamian civilization, had fallen to warrior tribesmen from the east, the Medes and Persians. The Medes and Persians were descended from the Aryan peoples who for centuries had been moving out of the grasslands of central Asia with their horses and herds. Some of the Aryans settled in the valleys and slopes of the mountains surrounding the great arid plateau between the Persian Gulf and the Caspian Sea. From them the region took its name, Iran, or land of the Aryans.

The Aryans who lived in the mountains northeast of Mesopotamia were the Medes, familiar to their prosperous neighbors as breeders of horses and as raiders of cities and trade caravans. Other Aryans settled south of the Medes, in the region of Parsa along the valleys, foothills, and plains of the Zagros Mountains, and these people became known

A PERSIAN GOLD MEDAL (400-330 B.C.)

as Persians. About 650 B.C., one of the Persian chieftains, Achaemenes, organized a small kingdom. His descendant, Cyrus, later brought the various tribes of Persians and Medes under his rule and led the united forces into Babylon.

Before Cyrus formed the Persian nation, a man appeared who would influence the Persians in another way. He was Zoroaster, or Zarathustra, who around 600 B.C. began to preach a new religion to the people of Iran. The Aryans had always worshiped many gods, especially Mithra the sun god, and they often sacrificed animals. The priests who supervised the many rituals became a privileged group. Among the Medes, these priests were known as the Magi. Zoroaster introduced no new rituals and started no new priesthood; he was a prophet and reformer.

Zoroaster was most active in eastern Iran, perhaps as a priest of the old Aryan religion, but he soon withdrew from society and went to live on a mountain. According to legend the mountain burned up, but Zoroaster escaped unharmed and began preaching his new faith. At first he was rejected by the priests and people, but finally he converted the prince Vishtaspa, who became his disciple and protector. From then on, Zoroaster attracted more and more followers.

For many years after his death, Zoroaster's wise sayings were memorized and passed on by word of mouth. Then they were written down as the sacred verses that made up the *Gathas.* Later came the sacred writings of the *Avesta,* but these were set down by priests who introduced new elements, such as miraculous tales about Zoroaster, and all kinds of rules and rituals.

CYRUS ENTERED BABYLON IN TRIUMPH.

The teachings of Zoroaster himself had been much more simple. He had spoken of Ahura Mazda, the god of light and truth and goodness. Ahura Mazda was engaged in a struggle with Ahriman, the god of darkness, falsehood, and evil. The struggle went on everywhere in the world and within all men. Zoroaster appealed to all men to help Ahura Mazda by their good thoughts, words, and deeds. In that way Ahriman would be destroyed, and evil and falsehood would be wiped out.

In asking all men to choose and act for good, Zoroaster introduced a new force into the religion of Iran. But the old gods and rituals did not disappear. In fact, the priests adapted many of Zoroaster's teachings to the old ways. At the same time, although Ahura Mazda was not the only god, he was the one the Persians were to honor above all others.

Until Cyrus appeared, the peoples of Persia were united by little more than their religion. Cyrus himself, so the legends went, was strongly influenced by the gods. A king of the Medes tried to kill him as a baby, but Cyrus was given to a shepherd couple who raised him until he was able to revolt and claim the throne. After uniting the Medes and Persians about 550 B.C., he went off to fight Croesus, the wealthy king of Lydia in western Turkey. A Greek oracle had told Croesus, "If you fight, a kingdom will fall." Confident, Croesus fought Cyrus, and indeed, a kingdom did fall— but it was his own kingdom of Lydia. Cyrus captured its capital, Sardis, and took control of Turkey, including the many Greek colonies along its coast. Before long Cyrus took more territories in Assyria and on the eastern frontiers of Iran.

Cyrus was a brave warrior who led his troops into battle, but he was no Assyrian tyrant, slaughtering and boasting. Instead, he was kind to the defeated enemy, and word of his generous ways soon spread. When he decided to take Babylon, many of its citizens, angry at their king's actions, welcomed him as a liberator. Rather than risk a battle at the great walls, Cyrus went to the side bounded by the Euphrates River. He had the water drained off into a ditch, so that his troops could walk across the riverbed and into the city.

CYRUS CONQUERS BABYLON

Cyrus lived up to his reputation; he did not allow his soldiers to loot Babylon. His finest act was to free the Jews in Babylon from their long captivity and see that they were safely conducted back to Jerusalem. By combining statesmanship with his conquests, he brought most of the old Babylonian empire under Persian control. He allowed the various peoples—Jews, Greeks, Babylonians, and others—to keep their own gods, customs, and local government, and these people repaid him with respect. His own Persians called him "Father," and they honored him with a great tomb after he died fighting at the eastern borders in 530 B.C.

Cyrus's son, Cambyses, fought many campaigns to hold the empire together, and even conquered Egypt, but he was a much more severe ruler than his father. Even many of his own people were discontented, and before he died, a Mede by the name of Gaumata had set himself up as king. Gaumata pretended to be the brother of Cambyses, and no one dared protest. Then Darius, a true relative of the royal family, claimed the throne. He killed Gaumata and put down various rebellions throughout his kingdom.

Darius claimed that he had been inspired to seize power by Ahura Mazda, and to let everyone know of this miraculous event he decided to have a monument. He chose a great cliff on the road that ran from the Iranian plains to Mesopotamia, and there he had gigantic figures carved in the stone. Darius was represented standing with his foot on Gaumata, while facing him were the other rebel leaders, their hands bound behind them. Above them all was the sign of Ahura Mazda. And to make sure that all people would understand, Darius had the story inscribed in three languages.

The inscription on the cliff began: "I am Darius, the great king, king of kings, king of lands peopled by all races, for long king of this great earth." This may have been an exaggeration when the carving was made, but it was certainly true before his reign ended. Through conquests and alliances, Darius built up a vast empire. In the north it extended from the Danube River in Bulgaria, across Turkey, and into the mountains and plains of central Asia. In the south it stretched from Egypt and the Mediterranean coast all the way to the Indus River in India.

Darius and his Persians managed all these lands

DARIUS AND AN ENVOY FROM MEDEA

63

with great skill. True, the Persians had taken over much from their subjects—great cities, fertile farmlands, roads, trade routes, business and administrative practices, laws, scribes, the cuneiform script. But the Persians were wise enough to encourage local customs, religions, languages, and officials. They knew how to borrow the best from all peoples and how to keep all peoples working together. And although the Persians had built up their empire by conquest, they ruled it with law and order, not with force and terror.

The empire was divided into 20 satrapies, or provinces. Each was administered by a satrap, or governor, usually a Persian noble who could expect to pass on his position to his heirs if all went well. Judges, military commanders, and tax collectors were appointed by the emperor. To keep all these officials alert, the "king's eye," or inspector general, made unannounced visits to the satrapies and reported back to the emperor.

Linking the empire was a network of roads, many of them well paved. One road, which ran from Susa to the Mediterranean, was about 1,600 miles long. Along the main routes were post stations, with horses and riders waiting to relay messages. Herodotus, a Greek who traveled through

the empire, reported that the riders "are stayed neither by snow nor rain nor heat nor darkness from accomplishing their appointed course with all speed."

Trade was international, with caravans bringing products to and from the widely scattered provinces. Business flourished, and there were even banks that made loans, but farming was still the most important occupation. The Iranian plateau was so dry that the farmers had to use a system of underground canals to irrigate their fields, and the Persians always depended on their provinces for many foods. Darius himself tried to introduce different plants and animals into various parts of the empire.

Each satrapy paid taxes or tribute, but for the most part the amounts demanded were reasonable. People were expected to give some work to public projects, such as roads, but there was no brutal slavery. Besides, there were laws to protect all men. Punishments could be severe, but everyone respected the laws of the Medes and the Persians.

The Lydians had invented coinage, but the Persians were the first to put it to wide use. While various local officials had the right to issue copper and silver coins, only the emperor could issue gold coins. Darius organized the economic affairs of the

THE MIDDLE EAST AND THE PERSIAN EMPIRE (600-525 B.C.)

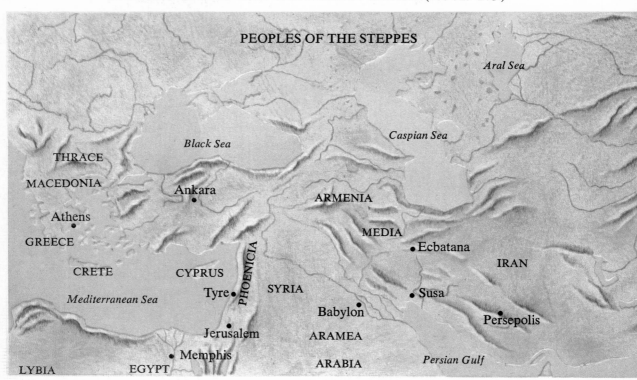

empire so well that some of his people secretly called him "the merchant."

To keep order, there were troops stationed throughout the empire. Originally the army had been made up entirely of Persians and Medes, but gradually it came to have mostly paid soldiers from its subject peoples. The Persians' navy was almost completely made up of Phoenicians and Greeks from the Mediterranean coast ports. Only Persians, however, could belong to the special royal guard, whose 10,000 members were known as "The Immortals." Trained from youth, the Persian archers mounted on horses could shoot arrows as they charged the enemy, and keep shooting as they rode off. Sometimes the Persians used elephants and camels in battles, and in desperate situations they attached sharp blades to their chariots and rode through the enemy's ranks.

DARIUS, KING OF KINGS

At the center of this great empire was Darius, king of kings. He knew his power, he used it, and he did not hesitate to remind his subjects of what they owed him. Yet Darius could hardly forget the ceremony by which he had been crowned emperor. At Pasargadai, a former capital under Cyrus, the priests presented him with the robe of Cyrus; after that he ate a peasant's meal, to remind him that he was a man like any other. This custom was followed by all the Persian emperors.

As his first captial, Darius had chosen Susa, the old capital of the Elamites, and there he built a great city with a citadel and palace. The materials came from all over the empire—timber from Lebanon, silver and ebony from Egypt, ivory from Ethiopia. Then Darius decided to build a capital that would be the most magnificent in the world. He chose the site of Persepolis, and there craftsmen from many lands worked during his reign. The project was so ambitious that work continued during the reigns of the emperors who followed.

On a great terrace, made of huge stones held by iron clamps, rose various buildings with dozens of tall, slim columns. On the walls were stone carvings that depicted long processions of people bringing tribute. Carvings lined many of the fine stairways. Other sculptures represented great winged and human-headed beasts like those in the Assyrian

SILVER AND GOLD PERSIAN KING (700 B.C.)

palaces. No other city of the time had such a handsome set of buildings, and Persepolis remained a special city for the Persian emperors. Religious rites and the work of government were carried on in other cities, but Persepolis was a ceremonial center for the emperors. There, too, they were buried.

As he sat in his magnificent palace at Persepolis in the closing years of his reign, Darius might well have thought that his empire would last forever. True, there were some minor disturbances, such as the revolt of the Greek cities along the Turkish coast, but he soon crushed them. Then, to show that the Persians intended to be masters of their world, he sent land and sea forces to punish the Greek mainland cities, Athens and Eretria, which

AMBASSADORS BROUGHT TRIBUTE FROM FOREIGN
NATIONS TO PERSIA AT THE ROYAL CITY OF PERSEPOLIS.

had aided the revolt. But storms wrecked the fleet, and all the army could do was campaign in the north of Greece.

Two years later, in 490 B.C., Darius still felt that the mainland Greeks were his empire's greatest threat, and he sent a great fleet with troops across the Aegean Sea. The Persians took islands along the way, captured Eretria, and then landed at Marathon, north of Athens. There the Persian soldiers were defeated in battle by a force of Athenians only about half their number. The Persians retreated to their ships and, after attempting some attacks along the Greek coast, sailed back to Asia.

To Darius and his Persians, Marathon was nothing but a minor battle they had lost. They did not realize that it was the defeat of an imperial army from the East by a group of free men defending their homeland. Within a few years after Marathon, the great Darius died. He had been all-powerful, but he had remained "a friend to his friends." To the Persians, he left an empire and a pride in themselves as a people.

Darius's son Xerxes was a far more cruel warrior and a far less able leader. Some of his counselors persuaded him to renew the campaign against Greece, but first he had to put down revolts in Egypt and Babylon. Meanwhile, his armed forces made preparations for a major expedition. Supply depots were set up in northern Greece, and a pontoon bridge was laid across the Hellespont where the Persian army had to cross from Asia into Europe. Finally, with a fleet of 1,000 ships and an army of about 100,000 men, the Persians set forth to show the Greeks who was master.

Xerxes himself led the Persian forces as they moved down through northern Greece. By 480 B.C. they were at the pass of Thermopylae, which led to the south; although thousands of Persians were killed by a heroic band of Greeks, the Persians continued to advance. They captured and burned Athens, but the Athenians had escaped to the islands and cities to the south.

THE DEFEAT OF PERSIA

Now only the Greek fleet stood between the Persians and total victory. Xerxes sat on a chair on shore to watch the battle off the island of Salamis, but the Persian navy was out-maneuvered and beaten. Xerxes was so furious that he had his admiral executed; when the other Persian sailors heard this, many of them fled with their ships. Xerxes hurried back to Persia by land, leaving most of his army in Greece.

The next summer, this Persian army was defeated at Plataea in Greece, while at the same time a Greek fleet defeated the Persians off the Turkish coast. This was followed by the loss of the Greek cities in Turkey and all of Persia's European territories. Having failed at building his empire, Xerxes turned to building colossal monuments at Susa and Persepolis.

In 465 B.C., Xerxes was assassinated, an event that signaled the breakdown of order throughout the empire. Satraps rebelled against the authority of the king of kings; Egypt revolted and broke free. Persia became involved with Athens and Sparta in a series of wars and shifting alliances, but lacked the energy to take command. Persia no longer depended on its archers riding into battle. Instead, it depended on gold coins to bribe various cities and armies to fight each other.

The weakness of the Persian empire was reflected in the quarrels within the royal circle. Once, the younger brother of an emperor tried to seize the throne, and to do so he hired an army of Greek soldiers. The younger brother was killed in battle, but the Greeks re-organized themselves and made their way through Persian territory back to Greece. Imperial Persia could not contain the disciplined Greeks.

In 359 B.C., Artaxerxes III came to the throne. For a while he seemed to be reviving the old Persian empire by his reconquest of Egypt and many of the old provinces. But Artaxerxes, who had murdered to seize power, was himself poisoned, at the very time that Philip of Macedon was taking command of the Greeks. It was Philip's son, Alexander, who finally defeated the Persians in a series of battles across western Asia. One by one the great cities fell, until even Persepolis was in flames. Darius III, the last king of the dynasty founded by Achaemenes, was killed by his own men after fleeing from Alexander's triumphant army.

Alexander never lived to see his dream of a united Greek and Persian world, and on his death the Persian empire was divided among his generals. The peoples of Iran would help to build other empires and take part in other civilizations. But the Persian emperors, for all their greatness, had failed to show their people how to govern themselves.

AN INDIAN CITADEL

Civilization Comes to India
3500 B.C.-200 B.C.

FOR thousands of years during the Stone Age, only scattered groups of people had lived in India. With only the simplest tools of bone, wood, and stone, they hunted and gathered food. Cut off from other peoples by the mountains and the sea, the first Indians made few advances in their primitive way of life. Then, sometime between 3500 and 3000 B.C., new settlers began to appear along the Indus River Valley in northwestern India, a region that would be called West Pakistan thousands of years later. It seems almost certain that these newcomers were from the mountains and plateaus to the northwest, the modern lands of Iran and Afghanistan.

When they arrived, the newcomers were already able to make pottery, to farm, and to raise animals. Most likely, too, some of them knew about the cities far to the west, on the plains of Mesopotamia. From those more advanced cities, the Indus valley people learned about new objects, such as copper and bronze tools. They also heard tales about how those distant peoples controlled the river's water, or how they scratched signs in clay tablets to record words. But however much they may have borrowed, the Indus valley people

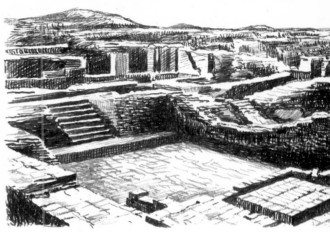

WORKERS' QUARTERS IN HARAPPA

THE GREAT BATH AT MOHENJO-DARO

worked out their own ways. By 2500 B.C., a distinctive civilization had begun to develop along the Indus River.

The river itself played an important part in this civilization. Sometimes it flooded so badly that it wiped out villages and fieldworks, or even changed its course entirely. Usually, however, it overflowed just enough to leave a rich soil for each season's crops, and the people worked together to take advantage of it. The river also made it easy for the various settlements to exchange goods and ideas.

THE PEOPLE OF THE INDUS

Of the dozens of villages, two soon grew larger than the others and became the centers of their regions. Far up the river was Harappa, with its great citadel and grain stores. Down river was the equally important city of Mohenjo-Daro. Led by these cities, the Indus valley people shared a way of life that was truly flourishing about 2000 B.C.

This civilization had little effect beyond the one small corner of northwestern India. Most of India was still inhabited by half-wild tribesmen who had little or no contact with each other. It was to be many centuries, in fact, before there was any real unity among the people of India, largely because of the geographic barriers. India was divided by a variety of landscapes and climates ranging from desert to jungle. The only condition common to all of India was the annual rainy season, which lasted from May to September.

There was a great difference between northern and southern India, and this was to have enormous influence on India's history. The north had variety in its terrain, but all its regions had at least some contact with each other. Across the far north were the forested slopes of the Himalayas. Spreading down from them were the northern plains, fertilized by the rivers from the Himalayan snows. Then came the great central plateau, and across its southern edge ran the Vindhya Mountains, which almost cut India in two. Below these mountains was southern, peninsular India, a world apart.

One of the things that set southern India apart from the north was its semi-tropical climate. Even more important was the isolation forced on the

THESE ENGRAVED SEALS FROM MOHENJO-DARO AND
HARAPPA WERE MADE BY SKILLED INDIAN CRAFTSMEN.

southern peoples by the Vindhya Mountains. The southerners came to be called Dravidians, after the language they spoke—a language totally unrelated to that of the northerners.

The Dravidians were largely unaffected by the Indus valley culture and kept up their own religion and social customs. In time, however, they came into contact with the northerners through trade; the northerners were anxious to buy gold, pearls, conch shells, spices, and other rare products from the south. Even so, it was a long time before the Dravidians became a part of Indian civilization, and some isolated tribes did not change their ways until modern times.

By 2000 B.C., the Indus valley people were thriving. They raised barley and wheat as their basic crop and grew cotton to be woven into cloth. Herdsmen tended the large humped cattle that provided food and drew the wagons. Hunters hunted animals such as the tiger, the rhinoceros, the crocodile, and the elephant, as well as smaller game. Along the river, men loaded rafts with produce to be traded in the Persian Gulf or to be paid as taxes to Mohenjo-Daro.

Mohenjo-Daro was hardly a center of luxury, but it was a prosperous and splendid city for its day. Like Harappa, it was dominated by its great walled citadel, built on a mud-brick platform many feet high. Within the citadel were the fine buildings of state and ceremony, including the Great Bath, made of stone and used as a pool in certain rituals. Also in the citadel was the large civic granary, where the harvest was stored in well-ventilated chambers. No one thought it strange to have the granary in the citadel, for the entire life of the community depended on the crops.

Below the citadel was the residential quarter of Mohenjo-Daro, where people went about their daily tasks. Women drew water from the many wells, while along the streets workmen cleaned debris from brick-lined drains. Metalsmiths made axes, knives, and saws from copper and bronze. Skilled craftsmen cut delicate figures of animals into small square stones that would be pressed into clay as seals. Some seals had words printed in a script made up by the Indus valley people, although they probably borrowed the idea from the Sumerians of Mesopotamia.

A TOY CART FROM
MOHENJO-DARO
(2600-2300 B.C.)

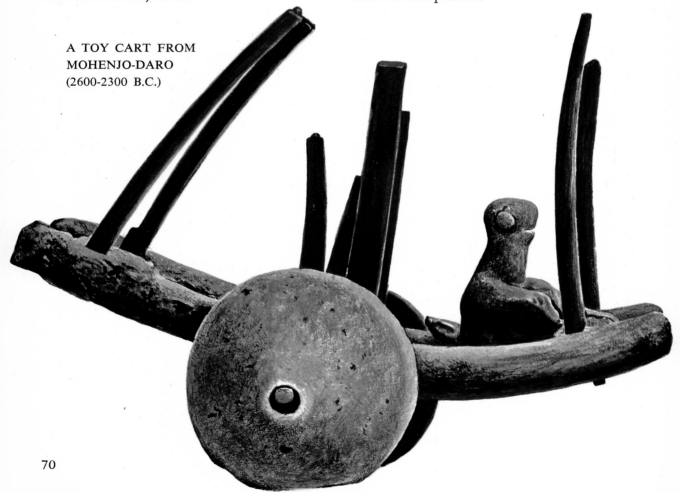

THE INDUS RIVER BROUGHT PROSPERITY TO THE PEOPLE OF ITS VALLEY.

All the houses were of plain design and made of mud-brick, but those of the wealthy had pleasant courtyards and staircases to upper stories. The most remarkable feature of the Mohenjo-Daro residential quarter was its careful planning. Streets crossed each other at almost perfect right angles, and buildings were arranged in blocks of more or less the same size.

Such organization did not mean that the rulers kept the people regimented by force, nor that they had to use force to unify all the Indus valley settlements. As did other civilizations that grew up along rivers, the Indus valley people found it easy to share their way of life. They believed that their rulers were responsible for the welfare of the community and that the gods were responsible for the fertility of nature. To keep harmony in this world, the people could also respect the need for an orderly city.

THE COMING OF THE ARYANS

As the centuries passed, however, the Indus valley settlements began to decline. Perhaps they exhausted their resources by letting their population grow too fast; perhaps they had become too fixed in their ways and no longer changed with the times. Then, about 1500 B.C., Mohenjo-Daro was attacked. It was a sudden raid, for some people were struck down in the streets and in their homes. Mohenjo-Daro was left forever deserted.

It is likely that the raiders of Mohenjo-Daro were the Aryans, the people who began to appear in northern India about this time. No one knows the original homeland of the Aryans; perhaps it was in central Asia or even far north near Scandinavia. For hundreds of years various tribes of Aryans wandered about parts of Europe and Asia. Although their name meant "kinsman," most of the tribes had long ago lost touch with each other. Their languages were related, however, and they shared the way of life of semi-nomadic warriors and herdsmen.

Whatever their original homeland, the Aryans who appeared in India were close relatives of those who had earlier settled to the northwest in the land of the Aryans, or Iran. The Aryans did not sweep across India and wipe out everything in their path. They took many years to move gradually eastward and spread along the river basins of northern India. During this time, some of the native people resisted and some retreated, but finally they had to go on living with their conquerors. Later, as the two peoples mingled, each influenced the other's way of life.

IN EARLY INDIA, LEARNED MEN, USUALLY PRIESTS, GAVE ADVICE
AND INSTRUCTED THEIR FOLLOWERS IN THE ARYAN RELIGION.

The Aryans set themselves up as an aristocratic warrior class, and the settled peoples were forced to work for them. Although they did some farming, the Aryans preferred to raise cattle, sheep, and goats for their food. They could also tan leather, work metals, and weave cloth. But most of all the Aryans liked to go out to raid and to battle, seizing booty or demanding treasures or food as tribute. They rode forth in two-wheeled chariots drawn by two horses, with a charioteer crouching low between two warriors armed with spears or bows and arrows.

For hundreds of years, the Aryans in India kept up their old ways. They did not even build cities, but lived in wooden houses in fortified villages. They had small assembly halls, where the elders discussed the affairs of the tribe, while the young men held chariot races outside the village. The Aryans enjoyed music, dancing, and feasting. Their favorite drink was *soma,* an intoxicating juice from a plant, and one of the men's favorite pastimes was gambling with dice. Not everyone approved of gambling, as shown by a song that said:

My wife rejects me and her mother hates me.
The gambler finds no pity for his troubles.

It was not surprising that the Aryans worshiped Indra, the powerful god of thunder and battle, although Indra was only the most important of the many gods they worshiped. Most of the gods were forces of nature, such as Agni, the fire god, or Varuna, the sky god. To show their devotion to the gods, the Aryans held many ceremonies around their altars. Often they sacrificed animals. Promi-

HYMNS AND PRAYERS WERE PASSED ON FROM GENERATION TO
GENERATION UNTIL THEY WERE COLLECTED IN THE *RIG-VEDA*.

nent in the ceremonies were the prayers and hymns
in which the gods were asked to fight off evil and
to do good for the worshipers.

For many centuries, these hymns and prayers
were passed on from generation to generation by
the priests who chanted them at the ceremonies.
Finally some learned priests decided to write them
down in the Sanskrit language. They collected more
than one thousand of these hymns in a book called
the *Rig-Veda*. Many were extremely beautiful and
expressed the Aryans' devotion in simple language.
One of the finest was the *Hymn to the Dawn*:

Arise! the breath, the life has reached us.
Darkness has gone away and light is coming.
She leaves a pathway for the sun to travel:
We have arrived where men prolong existence.

The *Rig-Veda* was one of the four books that
made up the *Veda*, a title that meant "knowledge."
The *Veda* was the Aryans' traditional and religious
wisdom, much of which had been passed on for
centuries by word of mouth before it was written
down. The *Veda* included not only religious hymns
and prayers, but still older folklore, such as spells
and charms. Not all the Veda was fine literature,
however, and much of it was difficult for anyone
except the priests to understand. As the centuries
passed, the priests also added passages in prose,
such as commentary on the rituals and laws. Later,
too, they added the sections of profound philosophy called the *Upanishads*.

The *Veda* was to have a great influence on Indian
thought and culture, but when first set down, it
meant little except to a few people along the north-

A SANDSTONE CARVING OF THE HEAD OF SHIVA THE DESTROYER (A.D. 600)

ern river valleys. There, by the year 1000 B.C., great changes were taking place. When the Aryans first appeared, for instance, their families were grouped into tribes, each governed by an elected Rajah and a tribal council. As the Aryans became more settled and grew in numbers, the tribal groupings developed into city-states and kingdoms. Although these expanding kingdoms sometimes fought each other, they brought some order to the land.

Meanwhile there had been a gradual shift of people and power to the east and south of the Indus valley. Along the Ganges and Jumna rivers, many settlements grew up in the years between 1000 and 500 B.C. Some, such as Kaushambi and

Rajagriha, became great cities with strong defenses. In central India there was Ujjain, a sacred city with fine buildings of stone and paved streets. And in the northeast, the Magadha Kingdom began to grow powerful; it was to be the center of many important religious and political forces.

THE RISE OF HINDUISM

By 1000 B.C., the pre-Aryan and Aryan cultures had also begun to blend. Out of this mixture was to come the classic Indian civilization. The Aryans continued to lord it over the pre-Aryan peoples, but, through the centuries, the Aryans were also influenced by the pre-Aryans. The heroic tales and legends of both peoples led to the creation of the great Indian epic poems.

One of these was the *Ramayana,* a long poem said to have been composed by the poet Valmiki about 550 B.C. It was written in the Sanskrit language and told of Prince Ramayana, who was driven into exile by his jealous stepmother. With his wife Sita, the prince had many adventures, and at one point had to be aided by the king of the monkeys. Finally he was able to share the throne with his stepbrother. The poem became familiar to all Indians, and Prince Ramayana himself came to be looked on almost as a god, the ideal man and savior of mankind.

The other great Indian poem was the *Mahabharata,* which included such a variety of compositions that it was like an encyclopedia of moral teachings. In it, for example, was the *Bhagavad Gita,* or "Lord's Song," a beautiful philosophical poem. The main epic told of a great war, whose climax was a battle lasting eighteen days. All the states and peoples of India were described as taking part in the battle, which ended in the destruction of almost everyone. Although based on stories of real wars, the poem was full of legendary and fantastic elements.

The *Ramayana* also combined imaginative tales, legends, myths, and history. Both the *Ramayana* and the *Mahabharata* had been passed on from generation to generation by professional reciters for centuries. Even after they were written down, many additions and changes were made, since they were not sacred writings like the *Veda.* As a result, there were old non-Aryan and early Aryan sections side by side with those of later periods. Altogether, a great number of reciters, poets, editors, and priests worked on the poems through many centuries. The priests were especially anxious to make the poems an expression of Hinduism.

It was in the centuries following 1000 B.C. that Hinduism emerged as the religion of India. Certain elements of Hinduism existed as far back as the first Indus valley settlements, but Hinduism really developed out of the religion of the early Aryans. Their primitive forms of worship had little resemblance to later Hinduism, but as time went on their nature gods became more refined and their beliefs more complicated.

Vishnu, for instance, was only one name of the sun god of the early Aryans. In Hinduism he became one of the major gods, and as Vishnu the Preserver he belonged to the *trimurti,* or "three-formed" god. The other two forms of the *trimurti* were Brahma the Creator and Shiva the Destroyer.

By 600 B.C., Hinduism was spreading through all Indian life and thought. Much of the growth of Hinduism was due to the influence of the priests, or Brahmins. The priests of the early Aryans had performed the ceremonies and chanted the hymns. By giving up worldly pleasures and devoting themselves to religion, the Brahmins had gained great respect. They were responsible for keeping alive the sacred texts, and over the centuries they developed the elaborate ceremonies and the rules of conduct for Hindus. The Brahmins thus became not only priests, but also teachers and lawgivers, setting themselves apart as a superior class.

IN SOUTH INDIA, DANCERS AND MUSICIANS TOOK PART IN RELIGIOUS CEREMONIES.

THESE SCENES FROM THE LIFE OF BUDDHA WERE CARVED IN STONE IN
THE FIRST CENTURY AND ADORN THE GREAT STUPA (TEMPLE) AT SANTCHI.

Social classes were becoming an important part of Indian life. There had already been different classes of people in the early Indus valley settlements, and the Aryans, when they appeared, set themselves up as a ruling class. Under the Aryans, society developed along more rigid lines, and people became fixed into different *varnas,* or classes. At the top were the Brahmins, the learned and priestly class. Then came the warriors and rulers. Traders, farmers, and skilled craftsmen formed the next class, and lower still were the mass of common laborers. Finally, there were the "untouchables"—such people as the half-wild tribes, the Dravidians of the south, and the workers who did the dirtiest jobs, such as sweeping.

Along with the class system, there developed the castes. A caste was a group of families who shared the same *dharma,* or code of conduct. The *dharma,* for instance, laid down certain rules for ceremonies and diets, and it was important for everyone to carry out his caste's *dharma.* When castes started they were not too rigid, but gradually hundreds of castes developed. Each one was closed to all except those born into it, and people were expected to marry within their caste. Not everyone in a caste necessarily held the same job, but they were all of the same social class.

The Brahmins supported the class and caste system because it helped to keep order in Indian society and was closely related to Hinduism. One of the basic beliefs of Hinduism was the law of *karma,* which stated that a man's future life depended on his past behavior. The Hindus believed that a person passed through many lives. The early ones may even have been as animals, but as long as each living being behaved properly, he kept rising through better lives. Hinduism thus encouraged people to accept their position in a class and caste

and not to try to change society. The important thing was for each person to carry out his duty, and then he would be rewarded in his next life.

Hinduism did more than discourage people from trying to improve their lot on earth; it urged them to turn away from the material things of this world. Perhaps this was the most important teaching of Hinduism. The spiritual ideal of the Brahmins existed outside the world of matter. Their ideal was an absolutely pure state, beyond nature, reason, and experience.

Such teachings were difficult to understand, but the Brahmins were satisfied to have it that way because the mass of Hindus came to accept things as they were. Not everyone, however, was satisfied with the established religion. Some people objected to the elaborate ceremonies and the animal sacrifices. A few men turned to the sacred writings, like the *Upanishads* or the *Bhagavad Gita,* which seemed to speak directly to the gods. Others felt that the best way to earn a better life in the future was to turn away from their present life, and they became monks who punished their bodies.

One man who tried to reform Hinduism was Vardhamana, later called Mahavira, or "Great Hero," by his followers. Born about 540 B.C., Mahavira became a monk, but after growing dissatisfied with that life, he traveled about preaching. He taught that everyone should behave humanely to everyone else and always obey the rule of *ahimsa,* or "non-injury" to all forms of life. And since everything—including plants, minerals, air, and fire—had a soul, man must take care not to injure them. A man should not walk at night, for instance, for fear of stepping on an unseen worm. Such beliefs required great self-control, but when Mahavira died about 470 B.C., he had thousands of followers, who became known as Jains.

BUDDHA, THE "ENLIGHTENED ONE."

It was during this period, too, that another man began to question Hinduism. He was Siddhartha Gautama, who was born about 560 B.C. He became known as Buddha, the "Enlightened One," because he was said to have passed through 550 previous births and lives before reaching his final life on earth. According to tradition, his noble father kept the young Siddhartha in a palace surrounded by luxury and amusements, so that he would not know about the sufferings in the world. Siddartha grew up, married, and had a son. When he learned about the outside world, he gave up his nobleman's life and went off to become a monk.

At first he exposed his body to great pain, but then he realized that a life of hardship was no better than a life of ease. "Better than matted hair and ashes," Buddha said, referring to the monks, "are truth and discipline." Buddha began to teach people to take the Middle Path between the ex-

STONE CARVING OF A
FOLLOWER OF BUDDHA

tremes of luxury and the monk's life. The goal was *nirvana,* freedom from all the desires, pains, and delusions of this world. Only when he reached *nirvana* did a man escape from the cycle of births and deaths; to reach this goal, Buddha taught that a person must follow the Eightfold Path of Salvation. But Buddha did not offer a religion of gods and ceremonies. His Eightfold Path of Salvation was meant as a guide to right living and right thinking.

When he started to teach, Buddha had only five disciples, but after forty-five years he won over thousands of persons to his way of thinking. At the age of 80, with several of his followers gathered about, Buddha lay down and died. His body was cremated, and for a while various followers quarreled over what should be done with the relics of his body. Finally they were placed in eight *stupas,* or relic mounds. Many people adopted the yellow robe of the Buddhist monk and spread his teachings.

At first, Buddhism and Jainism were rivals, yet they had much in common. Both came out of traditional Hinduism and accepted certain basic ideas, such as *karma* and rebirth. Both attacked the caste system and tried to appeal to the mass of people; their writings were even in the common language. Both were religions based on a way of life rather than on a belief in gods. Both considered life in this world as something temporary, and they rejected its pleasures. Both rejected the sacrifices of animals, too, and encouraged respect for animal life.

But there was an important difference between Buddhism and Jainism. Jainism accepted almost all of Hinduism, and so remained a Hindu sect, winning converts largely in India. Buddhism, however, broke away from Hinduism completely, rejecting the Brahmin priests, the rituals, the gods, and the *Veda.* As a result, Buddhism won most of its converts outside of India.

While Buddhism and Jainism were developing, other forces were at work in India. About 500 B.C., the Persian Empire had made the northwestern region of India one of its provinces. The capital was Taxila, a seat of Hindu learning. Although the Indians paid a large tribute in gold and provided soldiers to fight in Persia's wars, Persia did not bother the rest of India. But 150 years later, the Persian Empire was taken over by Alexander the Great. Finding himself on the edge of India, Alexander started across the mountains in 327 B.C., fighting off the hill tribes. The next year he crossed the Indus River and approached Taxila. The Rajah realized it was hopeless to resist and welcomed Alexander with gifts of thousands of cattle and the promise of troops.

All the other leaders of the region, except one, soon did the same. The king who defied Alexander was Poros, a giant of a man. Alexander had boats carried overland to the Hydaspes River, sailed upstream at night, and took Poros and his men by surprise. That day a great battle was fought on the plain along the Hydaspes; the chariots and elephants of Poros could not maneuver against the cavalry and bowmen of Alexander, and it ended in total defeat for Poros.

The wounded Poros, when asked how he expected to be treated, told Alexander, "Treat me like a king!" Alexander was so impressed by his bravery that he placed Poros in command of the region. Alexander then moved eastward, capturing territory and founding new settlements, until his troops became restless at being so far from home. Setting up twelve altars at the farthest point he reached, Alexander then took his army down the Indus to the sea. He had been in India less than two years.

No Indian of the time even mentioned Alexander in writing, despite his ambitious hopes of uniting the best of the Greek and Indian cultures. He had brought a number of learned men with him, and in time the civilizations of India and the Mediterranean had some influence on each other. But in Alexander's day there was a gulf between the two worlds. Alexander, it was said, once saw a group of Indian holy men. He sent one of his Greek aides to ask them about their wisdom. The holy men were sitting naked under the hot sun when the Greek delivered Alexander's request. "No one who wears European clothes could understand our wisdom," the holy men said. "You must sit here naked on the hot stones to learn."

Within two years after leaving India, Alexander died. When word of his death reached India, there were mutinies among the troops he had left behind, and the Indian states began to struggle for control. One of the Indian leaders was Chandragupta, who as a young man had met Alexander. Chandragupta seized the throne of the kingdom of Magadha, and in 322 B.C. founded the dynasty named after his clan, the Maurya. Soon he was ruling much of northern India from his capital at Pataliputra.

Megasthenes, a Greek serving as an ambassador, described the wonders of Chandragupta's court. The great wooden palace had pillars encased in flowering vines made of silver and gold. Chandragupta had a bodyguard of armed women. Each year there was a ceremony at which the king had his hair washed in public. For amusements there were chariot races, hunting, and dancing girls. At the same time, Chandragupta organized his empire, controlled taxes and irrigation, had a spy system, and enforced strict laws. When he died in 298 B.C., he left the first true Indian empire to his son Bindusara.

Little was recorded of Bindusara's deeds, yet he must have extended and strengthened the Mauryan empire. The southern tip of India remained isolated, and there were always hill tribes and certain

AN EARLY INDIAN VILLAGE

KING ASOKA UNITED THE INDIAN EMPIRE AND ESTABLISHED BUDDHISM.

sections that stayed independent. But when Bindusara's son Asoka took control in 269 B.C., he ruled most of India. At first Asoka led the life of a great king, hunting and feasting. Then, in 261 B.C., he made war against Kalinga, a state to the east. Asoka won, but a great many men were killed or taken prisoner. When Asoka saw what suffering his ambition had caused, he was filled with sorrow and regret.

"ALL MEN ARE MY BROTHERS"

Almost at once, Asoka began to change his way of life. He gave up hunting and eating meat and all such pleasures. He also lost his desire to conquer by force and set about to win over men's hearts. He asked other rulers to follow his new policy, and he warned his own officials to stop using torture and harsh punishments. He helped the poor and the weak, and organized aid for animals as well as for people. Everyone, Asoka said, should be allowed to live in peace, security, and joy. Repeating a statement of Buddha's, Asoka said, "All men are my brothers."

As part of his new life, Asoka had adopted the Buddhist faith. Hoping to convert others to Buddhism, he sent out missions of Buddhist monks, some of whom went as far as the former empire of Alexander in western Asia and Africa. He sent his own brother to bring Buddhism to the island of Ceylon, off southern India. And to clarify the Buddhist beliefs and writings, he called a council in his capital. Buddhism owed a great deal to Asoka, who helped to establish and spread the religion. At the same time, he never forced his people to adopt Buddhism and showed his respect for all religions.

While working to spread Buddhism, Asoka also kept a firm grip on his empire. He was a practical man as well as a religious one, and he was wise enough to realize that his peaceful policies were helping to keep order in India. He even had his laws and proclamations inscribed on stones and pillars throughout the land so that his people would be informed.

Under Asoka, India prospered, and his name came to be honored throughout Asia. When he died in 232 B.C., however, the great empire built up by his family was split between two of Asoka's grandsons. Then came a series of kings, none of whom was strong enough to unify the land. To the people of India, it made little difference. Their religion taught them that the struggles and victories of this world did not really matter, and they continued their age-old ways.

The Land of the Great Wall
4000 B.C.-A.D. 220

RITUAL VESSEL (1538-1078 B.C.)

FOR many generations, the ancestors of P'an Keng had considered themselves kings in northern China. Yet this family of kings, the Shang Dynasty, had never governed from a central capital. About 1380 B.C., P'an Keng decided it was time to set up a capital. He had found what seemed to be the perfect site at Anyang. Situated near a bend in the Yellow River, the fertile plains were ideal for farming and pasture, while the mountains behind it had timber and wild game. Only one thing remained: P'an Keng had to find out if the move was approved by the gods and his ancestors.

P'an Keng sent for a diviner, one of the wise men who could read the will of the spirits. Everyone consulted the diviners for help in making decisions, whether it was the king planning a battle or a farmer wanting to know when to plant. Usually the diviner used animal bones in which small oval pits had been drilled. The diviner would heat a bronze rod in a fire and touch its point to the side of a pit. The heat cracked the bone slightly, and by examining the size and angles of the cracks, the diviner interpreted the message of the spirits.

For special occasions, the diviner used a large piece of tortoise shell in place of bones, and the choice of a capital was such an occasion. P'an Keng began to ask his questions. "Should the capital be set up at Anyang?" "Was the dream a good sign?" "Does Shang Ti, the great god, approve?" "Will T'ang, founder of the Shang Dynasty, aid in this move?" P'an Keng was overjoyed to hear the diviner interpret the answer to each question as "Yes" or "Fortunate." This meant that the spirits approved.

Since this was such an important event, the questions and answers, and even the date, were inscribed on the shell, which was then stored with the royal records. P'an Keng did not appreciate how wise this was until years later, when some of his people complained about the move to Anyang. Then P'an Keng was able to remind them that they should not oppose "the Great Tortoise" or the bones that determined men's fate.

Anyang had been settled long before the Shang kings made it their capital. It had been one of many settlements that grew up during thousands of years throughout the vast area of China. The many mountain ranges, however, cut the early peoples off from one another, and each region developed in its own way.

In the deserts, steppes, and mountains that ringed China from the west and north, nomadic tribes raised horses and sheep. Southward from the great Yangtze River, thickly wooded hills and a semi-tropical climate made it easier for men to live by hunting and fishing. Even after rice was introduced about 2000 B.C., many years passed before the people of the south cultivated enough to support large communities.

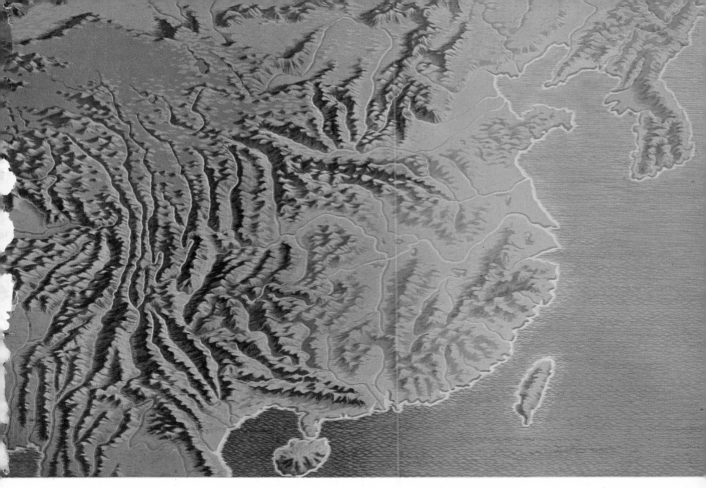

THIS RELIEF MAP OF CHINA SHOWS ITS MANY MOUNTAINS AND RIVERS.

The largest and most important settlements were on the great plain and in the highland valleys of the northeast. The rich soil there was easy to cultivate; it held moisture and was free of rocks. Each year the river rushed out of the mountains to the north and west and overflowed onto the plain. As it twisted its way eastward to the sea, the river left behind masses of yellow earth. Although the annual flood brought the soil on which the people's livelihood depended, it often wiped out dikes and villages. And so the people called the Yellow River their "great sorrow," even though they came to accept it and live with it.

EARLY COMMUNITIES

The first Chinese farming communities began about 4000 B.C. Millet was their basic grain, and pork their basic meat. Over the centuries, the people learned how to master the river somewhat, by draining and channeling; and as their harvests increased, their villages grew. By about 2000 B.C., these people were building small huts of clay, often round and with thatched roofs. Inside they made clay ovens, cupboards, and benches. They made pottery, too, and some of it was painted with handsome designs. And within a few centuries, these people were casting bronze and writing down their language.

For some of their advances, the Chinese were originally indebted to people to the west—perhaps as far as the lands bordering the Mediterranean. During thousands of years, travelers and traders from the West and the East had met in the desert oases and mountain passes of central Asia. There they exchanged ideas as well as goods. Whatever the Chinese learned from other peoples, however, they quickly adapted and made their own, so that the Chinese of later centuries no longer knew they owed much to the peoples of the West.

Instead, the later Chinese made up stories about their own great kings who had introduced civilization to their ancestors. Starting about 2850 B.C.,

81

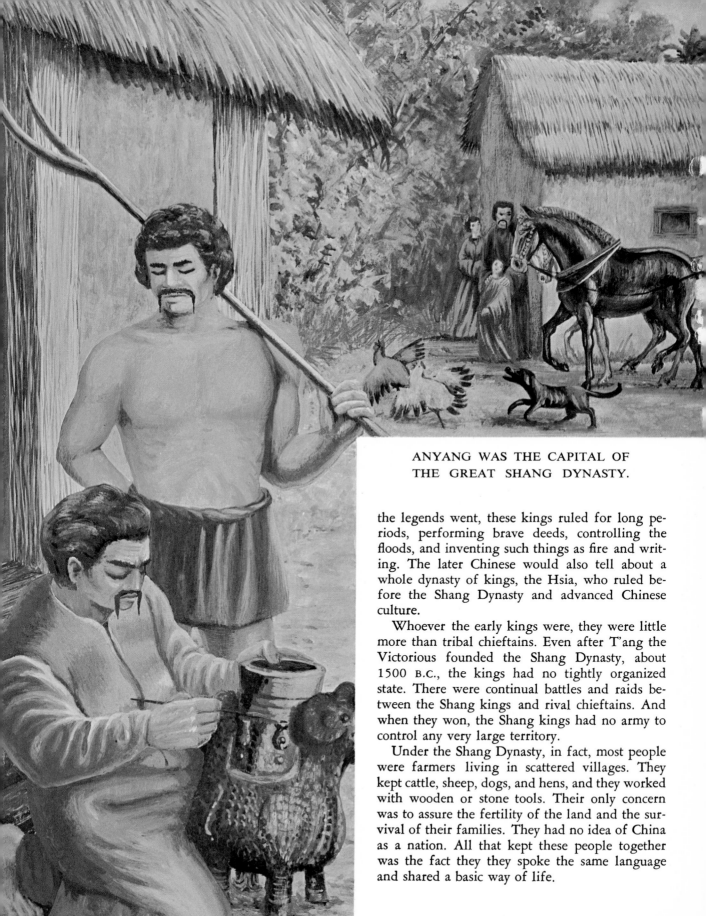

ANYANG WAS THE CAPITAL OF THE GREAT SHANG DYNASTY.

the legends went, these kings ruled for long periods, performing brave deeds, controlling the floods, and inventing such things as fire and writing. The later Chinese would also tell about a whole dynasty of kings, the Hsia, who ruled before the Shang Dynasty and advanced Chinese culture.

Whoever the early kings were, they were little more than tribal chieftains. Even after T'ang the Victorious founded the Shang Dynasty, about 1500 B.C., the kings had no tightly organized state. There were continual battles and raids between the Shang kings and rival chieftains. And when they won, the Shang kings had no army to control any very large territory.

Under the Shang Dynasty, in fact, most people were farmers living in scattered villages. They kept cattle, sheep, dogs, and hens, and they worked with wooden or stone tools. Their only concern was to assure the fertility of the land and the survival of their families. They had no idea of China as a nation. All that kept these people together was the fact that they spoke the same language and shared a basic way of life.

ITS PEOPLE INCLUDED PROSPEROUS MERCHANTS AND MANY CRAFTS-
MEN WHO MADE FINE POTTERY AND FASHIONED ARTICLES OF BRONZE.

Only in a few towns were people beginning to develop a Chinese culture. The towns were citadels of the ruling class, the nobles and warriors, and anyone with special skill or learning. The capital city, Anyang, was especially grand and came to be known as "the great city of Shang." It had a mud wall, and in the center of the city was the king's palace.

THE GREAT CITY OF SHANG

The upper classes in Anyang lived far differently from the people of the country. They had wooden houses built on platforms of beaten earth. Some of them had begun to use horses and owned small weapons and ornaments made of bronze. Their clothes were made of linen, wool, and furs. A few of the very rich even had silk, for Shang people had already started what would later be China's special industry.

A city like Anyang supported many craftsmen. Some carved fine statuettes from stone; some made beautiful pottery, even turning it on a wheel and firing it in a kiln. Perhaps the most respected craftsmen were those who made bronze vessels. Centuries before, some Chinese had learned the methods of melting and casting metal from peoples far to the west. By 1100 B.C., the Shang bronze workers could make vessels of many shapes and sizes, as well as fine bronze bells. They did such expert and beautiful work that the objects they created would never be surpassed.

These bronze vessels were in great demand among the upper classes of late Shang times. Their religion involved frequent rituals, and many of the ceremonies had to be performed with vessels of special shapes and designs. Foods and wines, for instance, had to be prepared and offered to the spirits in exactly the right vessel. This concern for doing things with elaborate precision was beginning to dominate the religion of the upper classes.

The king himself performed many of the ceremonies at court, while fathers presided at ceremonies within their own homes. The priests did little except assist at the ceremonies and consult the oracle bones. Among the poor and the peasants, the priests were more like magicians who could perform to assure fertility to the land. Although the lower classes did not have so many elaborate rituals, much of their religion also centered around the sacrificial ceremonies.

Sacrifices were made in temples and small chapels. The poor might offer only food, water, and wine in simple clay pots, while the rich used fine bronze vessels and often sacrificed whole animals such as sheep, pigs, or dogs. Some of the sacrifices were made to the gods present in every force and feature of the natural world. The earth, the wind, the rivers—all had their gods, and over them all was Shang Ti, the great god, "The Ruler Above." Shang Ti had special influence over battles and war, but he also gave good or bad fortune in such matters as raising crops.

ANCESTOR WORSHIP

Shang Ti was a very real god to these people, but most of the other gods were only vague, impersonal forces. Artists did not even try to paint or carve figures of them. Far more important than the gods, especially to the upper classes, were the spirits of ancestors. After a man died, his spirit lived on and became the guide and protector of his descendants. The ancestor's spirit lived with Shang Ti and had the power to give or withhold success, so the ancestors' spirits were honored and worshiped as gods.

The welfare of a family, and, indeed, of the whole nation, depended on making proper sacrifices to the gods and spirits. Human beings were even sacrificed on special occasions, such as the time just after the king had died, about 1050 B.C. Several neighboring regions were becoming rebellious, and the Shang nobles feared that they had not made the proper sacrifices. This time they would leave no doubt about their respect for the gods and spirits.

As usual, the rulers would sacrifice several prisoners they had captured in battle and made slaves. But perhaps this was not enough. The rulers then asked the diviners, "Shall we succeed in capturing barbarians from the west?" The oracle bone gave the answer:—"Yes." And so, while some men made preparations for the burial, warriors went off to raid for prisoners.

Outside of Anyang, the workmen dug another great pit in the burial ground of the kings and nobles. It was about twelve yards on each side and

AFTER THE DEATH OF ONE SHANG KING, MORE THAN 200 PERSONS WERE SACRIFICED AND BURNED ALIVE IN HIS TOMB.

about eight yards deep. At each end, ramps and stairs led down to the bottom, where a smaller tomb chamber had been dug out. This chamber was lined with wood carved in fine reliefs, inlaid with boar's tusk ivory, and decorated in several colors of lacquer.

The body of the king was laid in this chamber, and around him were placed bronze vessels, weapons, and royal treasures. Then, on various levels within the great pit, attendants and prisoners were sacrificed. Some were women wearing headdresses of turquoise; some were soldiers wearing helmets and weapons. Horses and chariots were buried, too. As workmen filled in the pit with earth, still more victims were buried. By the time the ceremonies were finished, more than 200 people had been sacrificed.

Despite this great sacrifice, the Shang Dynasty was losing its power, and not even the fine chariots of the king and his nobles could save it. These chariots, ornamented with bronze, were of some advantage on raids or in battles, but they were mainly for ceremony and display. There were not enough chariot troops, either, to fight off the restless border peoples, such as the Chou to the west. The Chou moved into the Shang territory and, by about 1025 B.C., occupied Anyang, the capital. Proclaiming their king as the "Son of Heaven," the Chou set up their own dynasty.

It was one thing to have a Chou king in the capital; it was another to get people throughout a vast territory to accept his authority. In a series of campaigns, the Chou gained control over some cities and tribes. Where necessary, they left one of their own people in command. For the most part, however, the Chou had to leave large regions under the control of the local princes. The most the Chou could hope for was that the local princes would take an oath of loyalty. In this way, the Chou kingdom became a feudal state.

At first, in the confusion that came with a new dynasty, there was a decline in the arts. But the Shang culture had become firmly rooted in the Chinese people, and they continued to make the fine bronze vessels. Religious practices remained much the same, too. The peasants, "the black-haired ones," went on believing in the many gods in nature, and they turned to the Wu, or magician-

OVER A PERIOD OF MANY YEARS, RIVAL CHIEFTAINS FOUGHT FOR CONTROL OF CHINA. ANY CHIEF WHO GAINED CONTROL USED THE CHOU EMPEROR AS A PUPPET.

priest, for aid in healing or magic spells. The upper classes and nobility still believed in the supreme god, whom they now called "Heaven," and still sacrificed to the spirits of their dead ancestors. The Chou also buried chariots in the great royal tombs. Unlike the Shang, however, the Chou did not sacrifice human beings.

Although the Chou were rugged warriors, they could not hold their feudal kingdom together. By 770 B.C., an alliance of rebellious states took the Chou capital, and the king was forced to settle at Loyang, a ceremonial city. Here the Son of Heaven was reduced to performing rituals and awarding honors to his various princes. He was a figurehead, and the feudal chiefs now held the real power.

But worse was to come in the next few centuries as the whole feudal system collapsed among the warring chieftains. Border states and hill tribes, northerners and southerners, new and old leaders—all competed for power. Any chief who gained control used the Chou king as his puppet. One chieftain even claimed to be king while the Son of Heaven still reigned. With so much disorder in the country, it was not surprising that families fought among themselves.

Meanwhile, a young man named Kung Fu-Tze, who later became known to the world as Confucius, was offering a new solution to the problem of governing China. He had been born about 550 B.C. in the small state of Lu, in the eastern province of Shantung. Although his father came of a good family, Confucius was poor as a youth and worked at various kinds of jobs. At the same time, he carefully observed the life around him and came

to have his own ideas about what had gone wrong in Chinese society. He became convinced that the way to restore harmony was for men to learn how to conduct themselves properly.

Many people in his day believed in proper conduct, or what they called *Li*. But these people interpreted Li in the narrow sense—the outward forms of ceremony or the strict rituals of sacrifice. Confucius was also in favor of proper ceremony, but he extended the idea to all men's relationships and behavior. In fact, it was better to miss some little detail in a ritual than to be discourteous to one's fellow man. Confucius saw *Li* as the proper conduct on which the harmony of civilization depended. The ideals of Confucius were to be just, kind, loyal, sincere, unselfish—in a word, to be humane. Men of good birth and learning might find it easier than other people to live up to these ideals, but it was only through proper conduct that a person became a true aristocrat.

THE TEACHINGS OF CONFUCIUS

Confucius held some minor position in the government, but he was too independent and had to leave the service when he was about 35 years old. To support himself, he began to lecture to anyone who would come to listen. Most of his listeners were young men, who soon became his disciples. Some were the sons of nobles and were accustomed to paying well for private tutors. Others were poor and could contribute only a little package of dried meat, but Confucius welcomed them all. It was not that he believed there was anything especially good in being poor. But poverty was nothing to be ashamed of as long as a man was trying to better his position in the world.

For Confucius wanted his pupils to remember that they were members of society. They must go out and live in the world, not retire from it. They were to be educated gentlemen, but they were to take an active part in reforming the government. The best government was one that brought about the harmony in which men could practice *Li*. Governments should never start a war, although people should fight if attacked. But fighting would never be necessary if all governments followed the rule Confucius preached to all men: never do anything to others that you would not want done to yourself.

Although Confucius wanted to reform the government, he was no revolutionary. He taught, in-

CONFUCIUS FOUNDED A RELIGIOUS PHILOSOPHY WHICH STILL EXISTS IN CHINA.

stead, that men should keep what was best in the old ways. Above all, Confucius wanted to restore the old loyalty to the family.

Confucius said little about the spirits of the ancestors or the gods, but he did not deny their existence. He accepted Heaven as a force in harmony with men who tried to live properly. For the most part, Confucius did not concern himself with religious questions. Once a pupil asked, "How should we serve the spirits?" Confucius answered, "You are not yet able to serve man. How can you serve spirits?"

Confucius attracted a number of followers, but during his lifetime he had little influence on the nobles who ruled the country. There was one nobleman, however, who admired Confucius, even though Confucius often criticized him sharply. The nobleman helped Confucius obtain an appointment to the Council of State, but when Confucius realized that he was expected to keep silent he resigned. Although he was now more than 50 years old, Confucius set out in search of some local ruler who would give him the opportunity to put his ideas into practice. For fourteen years he wandered from place to place, but in the end he had to give up his search. He returned to his birthplace, where he spent his last years, convinced that he was a failure.

Confucius died about 480 B.C., but his ideas did not die with him. During the next few cen-

turies, when China was split by the warring feudal states, many learned men took up the search for the proper forms of conduct. Some of these men held positions of influence, while others wandered about, lecturing to whoever would listen. Many began as pupils or believers of the Confucian teachings, but as the years passed they began to differ with one another. Each claimed to have the only correct interpretation of Confucius, and some even attacked his ideas. These teachers or their followers often collected their ideas in books, and since each was anxious to prove that his ideas belonged to the mainstream of Chinese tradition, they often invented history. They made up stories of wise ancient kings, for instance, in the hope of showing that their own ideas could be traced to the past.

CONFLICTING RELIGIONS

Curiously, the same spirit of questioning was alive in many parts of the world at this time. From about 600 to 300 B.C., many exceptional men arose to challenge the beliefs of their people. In India, there was Mahavira, the founder of Jainism, as well as the great Buddha. In Iran there was Zoroaster. The Jews had prophets like Jeremiah and teachers like Ezra. In Greece there were Socrates, Plato, and Aristotle. Some of these men were religious leaders, some were philosophers, some were teachers, and some were reformers. But all, in one way or another, were seeking to define man's goals.

In China alone there seemed to be a hundred different schools of philosophy competing for men's minds. For instance, Mo Tzu, who was born about the time Confucius died, founded the school of Mohism. Mo Tzu felt that the Confucians put too much emphasis on proper conduct, such as the long periods of mourning for a dead member of the family. Mo Tzu wanted to extend the ideal of loyalty and love beyond the family to all people. Yet his idea of universal love was not emotional. He condemned everything emotional, including music. Mo Tzu believed in discipline and organized his followers like an army. For a while Mohism had some influence, but it was too cold and extreme a philosophy to attract many Chinese.

Among those who opposed Mohism was Meng Tzu, who later became known as Mencius. Like many others, Mencius insisted that he was presenting the correct version of Confucianism. But because there were now so many competing schools of thought, Mencius had to argue and defend his ideas much more than Confucius had done. Many of Mencius's ideas were quite bold for his day. He claimed that man's natural instinct was to do good, just as water naturally flowed downhill. He called kings murderers because their actions so often resulted in the death of their subjects.

Still another school of thought was that of the Taoists. They claimed to base their beliefs on the ideas of Lao Tze, "the old master," although little was known about him. They took their name from the word Tao, meaning "Way." They believed that men should pursue the true Tao, which was beyond senses, reason, and actions. The Taoists encouraged men to withdraw from the world of affairs and to cultivate the natural, simple life. They rejected the idea that men should try to improve conditions on earth. Inner peace and happiness came before public duties.

The Taoists were in direct conflict with the Confucians, who believed that men could and should improve society. Confucians said that there should be no private satisfactions apart from public conduct. In time, Confucianism came to be accepted by the Chinese upper classes, although the appeal of Taoism always remained strong.

But neither Taoism nor Mohism nor Confucianism could save the Chou Dynasty, weakened by the centuries of struggle among its feudal states. In 256 B.C., the last Chou king gave up his throne to the feudal lord of the Ch'in. Unlike most of the other feudal lords, the Ch'in rulers had prospered largely through trade. Their prime minister was a former merchant, and it was his son Shih Huang who eventually seized power. By 222 B.C., Shih Huang and his supporters had gained control over the Chou kingdom and most of the former feudal states.

THE GREAT WALL

Shih Huang set about to do what had never been done in China—to gather all the various states and provinces into a single Chinese empire. He encouraged the old feudal families to leave their own territories and to come to the capital. While there, they felt flattered at being a part of the court circle, but Shih Huang appointed his own officials to run the government. He was careful to divide up the power among many officials, so that no one man could become his rival. By such clever tactics,

LAO TSE DIFFERED WITH CONFUCIANISM AND ESTABLISHED TAOISM IN ITS PLACE.

Shih Huang gained control over a vast territory.

In doing so, he made himself responsible for defending the empire. There was little threat from the south, but in the north nomadic tribes had been raiding the Chinese farming villages for many years. Walls had been built here and there, but they were of little use against the swift-moving hordes. Shih Huang gave orders for a great wall to be built across the northern boundaries of his empire. The small walls were to be improved and enlarged and then joined in one continuous wall. Thousands of Chinese worked on this vast project, and by 213 B.C. the Great Wall was completed. It extended for almost 2,000 miles and had 25,000 towers. Thousands of troops were stationed along its broad walks to keep guard.

Shih Huang and his supporters were not content with controlling the administration of the empire. They wanted to force a unity on it. Standard weights and measures were adopted, as well as a standard width for wagon axles, so that the wheels would fit the tracks in any road. The official philosophy of the government was that of the Legalist school, which stressed discipline and efficiency. The ideal man was the hard-working, uneducated peasant, not the wandering scholar who raised doubts in people's minds.

Shih Huang and his Legalist advisers began to look upon all other schools of philosophy—especially that of the Confucians—as dangerous. In

THE HUN INVADERS SWEPT PAST THE GREAT WALL AND ENTERED CHINA.

213 B.C., the government collected all the books in the empire. Books on practical matters such as medicine were set aside, and one copy of each of the classic philosophy books was saved in the State Library. All the other books were burned. The State Library was later destroyed, and scholars had to put together the classic books from what men could remember of them.

Although Shih Huang destroyed the books, he did help to reform the Chinese language. The Chinese spoke many dialects, some so different that they could not be understood by people from neighboring regions of China. Moreover, in the 1,200 or so years the Chinese had been writing down their language, the signs had changed in various parts of China. Originally most of the signs were based on pictures of familiar things; each sign or combination of signs represented a word. But now, all over China, the signs had developed different forms and were pronounced in different ways.

Shih Huang ordered that a uniform set of signs be adopted. Lists of correct words were issued, spelled in the basic script. All books, old or new, were to be written in this standard language. Shih Huang and his advisers changed the language because they wanted to make it more efficient, but the Chinese did not give up their idea that an individual's handwriting could be as beautiful as a work of art.

As he carried out his ambitious program, Shih Huang began to think of himself as a great leader. He called himself "First Emperor," convinced that there would be 10,000 to come in the empire he had created. The truth was that his chancellor and advisers had gained control of much of the power, while Shih Huang traveled about to be idolized by the people. And for all his efficiency, he was as superstitious as anyone else.

THE THREAT OF THE HUNS

On one of his trips, Shih Huang died. At once the empire was split by rivalries and rebellions, many of them led by people who resented the power that the imperial government had taken from them. In the end, the man who seized command was not from one of the old noble families. He was a rebel chieftain, Liu Chi, who entered the capital in 206 B.C. and declared himself emperor. Although he had still to defeat many other feudal lords, Liu Chi had established his own dynasty, the Han Dynasty.

Liu Chi had fought his way to the throne as an outlaw rebel, and he had no intention of allowing

90

WU TI DEFEATED THEM AND GAINED NEW TERRITORIES IN THE WEST AND SOUTH.

the old feudal families to regain their power. Instead, he put his own followers in charge of the various states and regions. He tried to make his officials responsible to his imperial court, where he ruled along with his ministers, but many of the states and regions went their own ways, becoming almost independent kingdoms. For the next 400 years, the Han Dynasty was to be torn continually between those who wanted strong local government and those who wanted a strong central authority. Only the most forceful men could impose their policies on the whole empire.

Wu Ti, who came to the throne in 141 B.C., was such a man, and he kept his power by leading the Chinese against their neighbors. In the north, for instance, there were the Hsiung-nu, or the Huns, nomadic tribes who had long been raiding the settled Chinese villagers. Even the Great Wall did not stop them, and now they were threatening the trade routes and lands to the west. Wu Ti not only drove the Huns back, but he also gained control over much of the western territory. In addition, he absorbed many of the southern peoples. Through trade and gifts, Wu Ti held his vast empire together, but the people resented the heavy taxes to support his wars, his gifts, and his court. When he died in 86 B.C., the emperor was once again reduced to being a figurehead.

Almost a century passed before another strong emperor came to power—the ambitious, clever Wang Mang. Although he was not in the direct line of succession, he forced the Han emperor to give up the throne to him. He invented a ceremony in which the imperial seal, a precious stone, was handed over to him, so that he appeared to be taking power legally.

Wang Mang pretended to be a progressive reformer and a friend of the people, but economic conditions soon became worse than ever. Finally there was an uprising led by the Red Eyebrows, a secret society of men who painted their eyebrows. Many groups joined in the rebellion, and they captured the capital. Wang Mang refused to flee. He was sitting on his throne in his imperial robes when a soldier entered and cut off his head.

THE GENTRY

During these years of conflict, it often seemed as though China would collapse. And perhaps it would have, were it not for the gentry, the people who owned the land and large estates. Some of the gentry were from old feudal and noble families, while others came from the new merchant class, but all shared the desire to keep order. Some of the gentry stayed on their estates to supervise the work and collect taxes, while others took positions with the imperial or provincial governments. The gentry could also afford to support some members of their families as educated scholars.

By intermarriage and cooperation, the gentry retained their privileges and influence, with some gentry families keeping power in their region for hundreds of years. Even when an examination system was set up to select officials, the gentry controlled it. They made up the tests, and their sons were the best educated persons in China. Besides, the examinations were not designed to test who would be most capable or efficient in a job. The tests were to see who had the proper attitudes of the Confucian gentleman.

THE GROWTH OF CULTURE

The teachings of Confucius were now accepted as the ideals of the upper classes, who were anxious to keep alive the traditions of the old aristocratic class. Confucius had said that the proper society would be run by humane, responsible men, and the gentry saw themselves as just such men. Confucianism became their official code. The poor masses of Chinese, however, found little satisfaction in Confucianism; they needed something that would help them endure the hardships of their life on earth. They found it in Buddhism, the Indian faith which reached China by the end of the first century B.C.

The gentry had no difficulty in accepting their life; it was a good one. They had fine homes and entertained their families and guests at banquets with acrobats and musicians. To visit friends or conduct affairs, they were rowed up and down the rivers and canals in sampan boats with little deck houses. In their leisure they gathered for poetry readings or painted for their own pleasure. They considered anyone who made his living by painting to be a mere craftsman.

No matter how the gentry looked down on them, the craftsmen of Han times kept up the Chinese traditions of artistic workmanship. The metalworkers made elaborately decorated vases, bells, and ornaments. The jade-carvers turned out delicate figures and designs. Certain Han craftsmen excelled in making lacquered objects, such as mirrors, toilet boxes, and bowls. Before the Han period, artists had usually based their decorations on fantastic shapes and geometric forms. Now

artists began to take an interest in natural forms. They began to depict animals and people in bronze and jade carvings, on tomb walls, and on lacquer boxes.

Literature also flourished in Han times. At the imperial court, poets were encouraged to write in praise of the emperor. Singers and dancers from southern China introduced lovely poems and songs. Scholars copied and edited the Confucian texts and other classics with their newly invented ink and paper. Some texts were engraved on stone so that rubbings could be made and one standard version would circulate.

The gentry were anxious to learn, and encyclopedias appeared in which everything known at the time was collected. *The Book of the Mountains and Seas* related animals, plants, and myths to the geography of the known world. *Shih Chi,* the first history, was filled with everything from biographies to astronomy, music, and economics. In their scientific writings, the Chinese did not show any special interest in searching for the basic laws of the natural world. Instead, they were more interested in practical inventions, just as their wise men had always been interested in improving society.

THE DIVIDED EMPIRE

In spite of the high level of their culture, the Han people were unable to govern themselves. At the imperial court, various groups competed to gain influence over weak emperors. The land was split by warring lords and generals, and the mass of people was forced to fight and pay taxes. About A.D. 184, a popular uprising was led by the Yellow Turbans, a religious sect. This was soon put down, but in its place came more feuding generals. By A.D. 220, the last Han emperor gave up the throne, and China was divided into three kingdoms. What remained were the people—the scholars with their books, the gentry on their estates, the artists and craftsmen with their materials, the peasants in the fields. Only they would hold China together until the next great dynasties appeared.

COURT LIFE WAS HIGHLY CIVILIZED UNDER THE HAN DYNASTY. LITERATURE, MUSIC, ART, AND THE DANCE FLOURISHED; FORMAL SCIENCE AND ECONOMICS THRIVED.

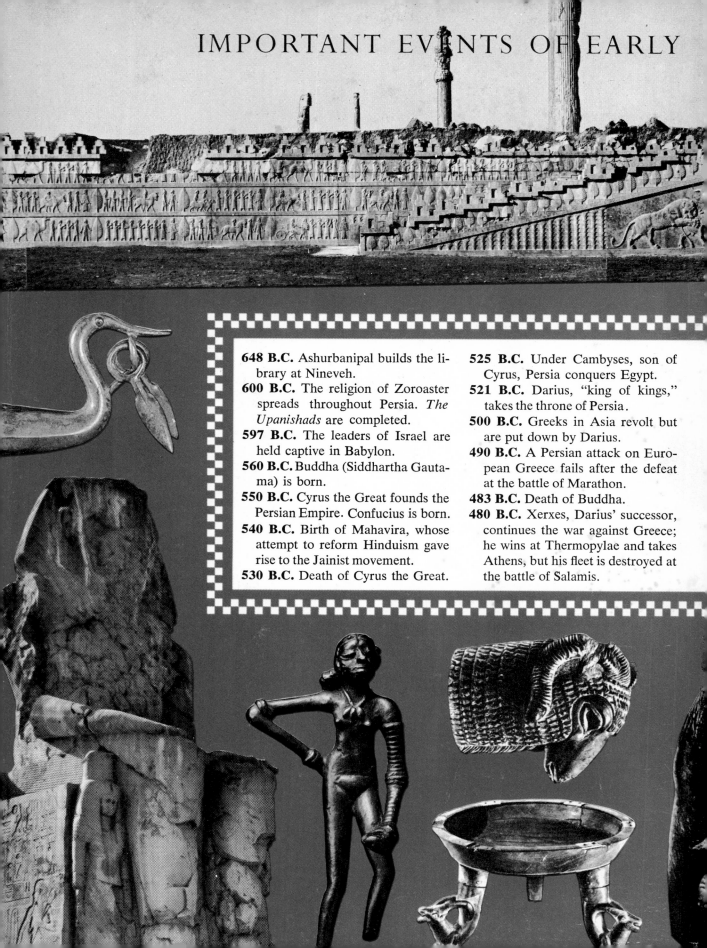

648 B.C. Ashurbanipal builds the library at Nineveh.

600 B.C. The religion of Zoroaster spreads throughout Persia. *The Upanishads* are completed.

597 B.C. The leaders of Israel are held captive in Babylon.

560 B.C. Buddha (Siddhartha Gautama) is born.

550 B.C. Cyrus the Great founds the Persian Empire. Confucius is born.

540 B.C. Birth of Mahavira, whose attempt to reform Hinduism gave rise to the Jainist movement.

530 B.C. Death of Cyrus the Great.

525 B.C. Under Cambyses, son of Cyrus, Persia conquers Egypt.

521 B.C. Darius, "king of kings," takes the throne of Persia.

500 B.C. Greeks in Asia revolt but are put down by Darius.

490 B.C. A Persian attack on European Greece fails after the defeat at the battle of Marathon.

483 B.C. Death of Buddha.

480 B.C. Xerxes, Darius' successor, continues the war against Greece; he wins at Thermopylae and takes Athens, but his fleet is destroyed at the battle of Salamis.

CIVILIZATIONS 648 B.C. - A.D. 220

465 B.C. Xerxes is assassinated.

359 B.C. Artaxerxes III becomes king of Persia.

334 B.C. After subduing and uniting the Greek cities, Alexander the Great crosses the Hellespont to attack the Persian Empire.

333 B.C. Alexander defeats the Persian army at Issus; Darius sues for peace and then flees.

327 B.C. Alexander the Great conquers India.

323 B.C. Alexander dies at Babylon.

269 B.C. King Asoka brings most of India under his rule.

230-221 B.C. Golden Age of Philosophy in China.

222 B.C. Shih Huang gains control of China and encourages trade. Chandragupta founds the Gupta Dynasty and rules India.

213 B.C. The Great Wall of China is completed.

206 B.C. The Han Dynasty is founded in China.

100 B.C. Buddhism reaches China and rapidly spreads among the lower classes.

A.D. 220 The Chinese Empire is split into three separate kingdoms.